PRACTICAL HANDBOOK ON FAIR LENDING FOR BANK DIRECTORS AND EXECUTIVE OFFICERS

AMERICAN ASSOCIATION OF BANK DIRECTORS

David Baris
Andrea K. Mitchell
Lori J. Sommerfield
Shara M. Chang

BuckleySandler LLP
Affirm, Inc.

Practical Handbook on Fair Lending
For Bank Directors and
Executive Officers

2016

Copyright ©

American Association of Bank Directors

American Association of Bank Directors
National Capital Office
1250 24th Street, NW, Suite 700
Washington, DC 20037

www.AABD.org

ISBN-13: 978-1530689408

ISBN-10: 1530689406

ACKNOWLEDGEMENTS

I wish to thank my colleagues at BuckleySandler LLP who dedicated their time and energies to developing this book: my co-authors Andrea K. Mitchell and Lori J. Sommerfield, as well as Jeff Naimon, who provided invaluable edits and feedback, MJ Kirsh, who meticulously proofread and cite-checked our copy, and Ashley Stockwell, who assisted in the formatting and publication of the book. I would also like to thank co-author and former colleague Shara M. Chang for her work on this project while at BuckleySandler and Affirm.

David Baris, President
American Association of Bank Directors

ABOUT BUCKLEYSANDLER LLP

BuckleySandler LLP provides premier legal counsel to protect and support the nation's leading financial services institutions, corporations, and individual clients. With more than 150 lawyers in Washington, DC, Los Angeles, New York, Chicago and London, it offers a full range of litigation, transactional, compliance, and regulatory services. "The best at what they do in the country." (Chambers USA).

ABOUT AFFIRM, INC.

Affirm, Inc. was founded by Max Levchin, founder and former CTO of PayPal, to help provide improved access to credit around the world. The company has the team that built the financial and anti-fraud technology at PayPal and Palantir and now is using it to build a credit network and underwriting system for the 21st century. Affirm reaches a broader population of consumers through advanced technology and analytics that look beyond traditional credit factors.

PRACTICAL HANDBOOK ON FAIR LENDING FOR BANK DIRECTORS AND EXECUTIVE OFFICERS

TABLE OF CONTENTS

                                                  Page

Chapter I.   Introduction 1

Chapter II.   Your Role in overseeing Fair Lending Risk...12

    A.   Board and Management Oversight........12

    B.   Asking the Right Questions................15

    C.   Hiring or Developing a Fair Lending Officer......................................18

    D.   Fair Lending Program Resources.........20

    E.   Integration of Responsible Lending Concepts into Fair Lending Programs....20

Chapter III.   What Types of Lending Discrimination Violate the Fair Lending Laws?..............22

    A.   Overt Discrimination........................22

    B.   Disparate Treatment........................22

    C.   Disparate Impact........................... 23

    D.   Redlining, Reverse Redlining, and Steering.....................................26

Chapter IV.   Where Does Fair Lending Risk Lie?.........31

    A.   New Product Development.................32

    B.   Advertising and Marketing.................33

    C.   Loan Origination.............................34

        1.   Mortgage Lending...................34

        2.   Auto Lending........................37

        3.   Unsecured Lending..................39

        4.   Credit Cards........................40

        5.   Student Lending....................42

        6.   Overdraft............................43

    D.   Servicing, Loss Mitigation, and REO 44

Chapter V.   Spotting "Red Flags" For Fair Lending Risk..46

Chapter VI.   Fair Lending Risk Management – How Strong Is Your Bank's Program?...............51

    A.   A Fair Lending Policy Is Critical...........51

    B.   Fair Lending Program Elements............51

        1.   Risk Assessment....................51

	2.	Preventive Controls.....................52
	3.	Detective Controls......................53
	4.	Issue Identification and Corrective Action 54
	5.	Reporting to Risk Management Committees..............................55
	6.	Consumer Complaint Management...55
	7.	Periodic Internal Audits.................56
Chapter VII.		Effectively Preparing For and Managing A Fair Lending Examination 58
A.		How to Effectively Prepare for a Fair Lending Examination.......................................59
B.		How to Effectively Manage the Fair Lending Examination Process.............................62
C.		"Soft" Exit Meeting.............................63
D.		What to Do After the Regulators Have Left...64
E.		"Official" Exit Meeting.........................64
Chapter VIII.		HMDA – Getting It Right And Knowing Your Data...66
A.		HMDA Compliance Requirements............67
	1.	Data Collection, Reporting, and Public Disclosure..............................67
	2.	Data Accuracy...........................68
	3.	Enforcement of HMDA and Regulation C...69
B.		Supervisory Use of HMDA Data...............71
	1.	Fair Lending Examinations............71
	2.	Transactions Requiring Supervisory Approval.................................73
C.		Public Use of HMDA Data.....................74
	1.	Private Litigation.......................74
	2.	Community Group Action..............75
D.		The Future of HMDA Data.....................77
Chapter IX.		An Introduction to Fair Lending Statistical Analyses – Making Sense of Your Bank's Data..79
A.		Why Your Bank Should Consider Conducting Fair Lending Statistical Analyses..............79

B. Collection and Use of Data for Fair Lending Statistical Analyses...................................81
    1. Using HMDA Data..................82
    2. Using Other Data Sources.........83
C. Using Statistical Analyses to Assess Your Bank's Fair Lending Performance...........84
    1. Understanding the Types of Fair Lending Reviews....................84
    2. Using Statistical Analyses Across Your Bank's Credit Administration Process...............................90
    3. What Should Be Done With the Results of Your Bank's Statistical Analyses?......................................93
D. Who Should Perform Your Bank's Statistical Analyses? 94

Chapter X. What To Do If Your Bank Becomes The Target of a Fair Lending Investigation or Enforcement Action........................…......97
A. How Fair Lending Investigations and Enforcement Actions Arise — and What to Expect....................................97
B. Choosing the Right Defense Team......100
C. Your Board Must Stay Apprised of the Proceedings................................101
D. What Is the Right Defense Strategy?.....102
E. Opportunity to Mitigate Risk.............104

APPENDIX A: FAIR LENDING LAWS & REGULATIONS

APPENDIX B: REGULATORY REFERENCE MATERIALS

APPENDIX C: CURRENT AND NEW HMDA REPORTING REQUIREMENTS

AUTHOR BIOGRAPHIES

ENDNOTES

PREFACE

To our knowledge, this book is the first of its kind – a reader-friendly, practical handbook on how boards of directors can provide adequate oversight for fair lending risk while explaining best practices to enhance your bank's fair lending compliance program and meet regulatory expectations.

When we began drafting this book, my original vision was for it to be approximately 20-25 pages in length, designed exclusively for outside bank directors so that they could read it casually while sipping a pina colada poolside. That kind of book is still possible, but as a sequel to this book.

We decided that the more immediate need was to reach a broader constituency in each bank because the topic of fair lending is very complex with nuanced distinctions and constantly evolving regulatory expectations. Therefore, this book will be a great resource not just for bank directors, but also for many others within your organization, including the chief executive officer, chief risk officer, chief compliance officer, and fair lending officer, and their respective staffs.

For those directors who cannot find the time to read the book in its entirety, they may wish to read some portion of it. To help guide you, we suggest that each director start by reading Chapter I, with a focus on the section entitled "Why Every Bank Director Should Read This Handbook."

In addition, the board of directors may consider designating one member of the board who is a member of the risk or compliance committee to read the entire book and become the resident "expert" on fair lending who can then share his or her knowledge with the board.

The chief executive officer may also wish to read some portions of the book, but those who are responsible for day-to-day fair lending program management (which may be the chief compliance officer or fair lending officer) should strongly consider reading the book in its entirety. Although some chapters may be worth a skim for certain topics with which compliance professionals are already familiar, other chapters may be worth reading on an in-depth basis (such as "HMDA – Getting It Right and Knowing Your Data" or "An Introduction to Fair Lending Statistical Analysis – Making Sense of Your Bank's Data"). The book can also serve as a helpful daily reference guide for particular issues – for example, how is disparate impact defined or how do regulators identify redlining practices?

We hope this book will be a useful resource for your organization.

David Baris
President
American Association of Bank Directors

CHAPTER I.
INTRODUCTION

Although the concept of fair lending has existed since the late 1960s, in recent years the industry has witnessed a dramatic shift in the regulatory landscape for enforcement of the federal fair lending laws. Non-compliance with fair lending laws — as well as allegations that a bank's lending practices are discriminatory — can damage a bank's reputation, lead to regulatory and litigation risks, and be costly to defend.

As a bank director, you need to be engaged in overseeing your bank's fair lending compliance efforts. That does not mean that you need to learn all of the technical details of fair lending, but you should have or gain a basic understanding of fair lending as well as an understanding of the role of the board of directors in overseeing your bank's efforts to comply with the fair lending laws.

That is the objective of this book.

As bank directors with many responsibilities, we know that you may not have the time to read this book entirely. However, while we strongly recommend that you each read at least Chapters I and II (eleven pages altogether), someone on your board or in management should read the book in its entirety and be in a position to address issues raised in the book with the board or a board committee. We also strongly recommend that your chief compliance officer and/or fair lending officer read the entire book.

What Is Fair Lending?

With the enactment of the Fair Housing Act in 1968 and the Equal Credit Opportunity Act in 1974, Congress declared lending discrimination in the U.S. illegal. The term "fair lending" was not defined by statute, however, until enactment of the Dodd-Frank Wall Street Reform and Consumer Protection Act of 2010 ("Dodd-Frank Act"). Under the Dodd-Frank Act, fair lending means "fair, equitable, and nondiscriminatory access to credit for consumers."[1]

The purpose of the fair lending laws is to prevent discrimination in lending on certain prohibited bases, as explained later in this book. Fair lending differs from, but is complementary to, responsible lending, which conceptually concerns economic and procedural fairness and transparency in dealing with consumers.[2]

What Are the Primary Federal Fair Lending Laws?

The federal fair lending laws include the Equal Credit Opportunity Act ("ECOA"), which is implemented by Regulation B and prohibits discrimination in extensions of credit for consumer and business purposes, and the Fair Housing Act ("FHA"), which is implemented by regulations of the U.S. Department of Housing and Urban Development ("HUD") and prohibits discrimination in residential real estate-related transactions. More background on these laws can be found in Appendix A. The states also have enacted anti-discrimination laws.

What Does a Fair Lending Allegation Look Like?

Fair lending enforcement actions and lawsuits allege unfavorable treatment of an applicant or a borrower on a prohibited basis (*e.g.*, race, ethnicity, gender, age, national origin) in some aspect of a credit transaction under either ECOA or the FHA.

ECOA applies to both consumer and business credit products, including mortgage loans, credit cards, auto loans, student loans, and other non-mortgage loan products.

The FHA applies to "residential real estate-related transactions," which includes mortgage lending for first and second liens.

Because ECOA and the FHA both apply to mortgage lending, plaintiffs often cite violations of both laws when bringing lawsuits or enforcement actions related to alleged discrimination in mortgage lending. However, Plaintiffs may only recover under one of those statutes.

Fair lending obligations apply to all aspects of a bank's credit-related activities for the entire life cycle of a product, including product development, advertising and marketing, taking and processing applications, underwriting, pricing, servicing, collections, loss mitigation, and repossession and foreclosure.

Why Fair Lending Should Be Among Your Bank's Top Compliance Priorities

Federal government agencies with fair lending supervisory and enforcement authority have become increasingly active in pursuing efforts to enforce the federal fair lending laws through their supervision, examination, and enforcement activities, resulting in numerous public and non-public settlements. The U.S. Department of Justice ("DOJ") reported that, in 2014 alone, it oversaw the distribution of over $500 million to consumers in connection with fair lending settlements dating back to 2010.[3]

Unprecedented Enforcement Actions in the Mortgage Industry

Since 2010, several major banks have entered into the largest mortgage fair lending settlements in history.

For example, in December 2011, DOJ entered into its largest fair lending settlement ever — totaling approximately $335 million — to resolve allegations that Countrywide discriminated against African American and Hispanic borrowers by charging higher fees and interest rates on residential mortgage loans, and steering such borrowers into subprime mortgages from 2004 to 2008.[4]

In July 2012, DOJ announced its second largest fair lending settlement — totaling approximately $175 million — in a case involving Wells Fargo Bank with similar mortgage pricing discrimination allegations.[5]

Significant Enforcement Actions for Auto and Other Non-Mortgage Credit

Sizable fair lending settlements have also occurred in non-mortgage lending contexts.

To illustrate, in December 2013, the Consumer Financial Protection Bureau ("CFPB") and DOJ entered into consent orders with Ally Bank and Ally Financial (together, "Ally") requiring Ally to pay $80 million in damages to presumed African American, Hispanic, and Asian/Pacific Islander borrowers who allegedly paid higher dealer mark-up on their auto loans than presumed non-white Hispanic borrowers, as well as $18 million in civil money penalties.[6] Dealer mark-up is the amount by which an auto dealer may mark up the interest rate above an indirect auto lender's risk-based buy rate based on the lender's discretionary pricing policy.[7]

In June 2014, DOJ and the CFPB entered into the federal government's largest credit card discrimination settlement in history — totaling $169 million — to resolve allegations that Synchrony Bank, formerly known as GE Capital Retail Bank, denied Hispanic borrowers the opportunity to participate in credit card debt-repayment programs by excluding from its direct mail campaign customers with a mailing address in Puerto Rico and customers who requested to receive communications in Spanish.[8]

Fair Lending Must Be a Key Regulatory Focus for Banks of All Sizes

Recent trends indicate that regional or community banks are no better insulated from fair lending enforcement actions than large national retail banks.

To illustrate, in September 2012, Luther Burbank Savings entered into a settlement with DOJ for $2 million to resolve allegations that the bank's $400,000 minimum residential mortgage loan amount policy adversely impacted African American and Hispanic borrowers, and residents of majority-minority census tracts throughout California.[9]

In March 2013, Community First Bank, a $7 million bank based in Pikesville, Maryland, entered into a settlement with the Office of the Comptroller of the Currency ("OCC") to resolve a rare reverse discrimination claim.[10] The OCC alleged that Community First Bank's mortgage lending program, which provided lender credits to women and minorities, resulted in more costly loans to the bank's white and married borrowers. Under this settlement, the bank was required to pay $73,000 in restitution to 64 borrowers.

Private Fair Lending Litigation Is Alive and Well

Private plaintiffs and consumer advocacy organizations have also actively pursued fair lending claims by filing administrative complaints with federal government agencies and individual lawsuits and class actions against banks.

For example, in *Ramirez v. Greenpoint Mortgage Funding, Inc.*,[11] three minority consumers in California who had obtained mortgage loans from GreenPoint successfully brought a class action on behalf of other Hispanic and African American borrowers alleging that GreenPoint violated the federal fair lending laws because its discretionary pricing policy led to a higher likelihood of loan officers charging protected class borrowers disproportionately high rates, points, and fees, and increased the average cost of mortgage loans to minorities. GreenPoint resolved the allegations by paying $14.7 million to harmed borrowers in 2011.

In addition, over the last five years, the National Fair Housing Alliance ("NFHA") has conducted investigations relating to the maintenance and marketing practices of real estate owned ("REO") properties owned by several lenders and servicers in major metropolitan cities nationwide.[12]

Based on the findings of these investigations, NFHA filed jointly with HUD complaints against several banks and Fannie Mae on the basis that their REO properties in minority communities were not maintained and marketed in the same manner as properties located in majority white areas.

The first of these complaints was filed against Wells Fargo in April 2012. In June 2013, HUD and Wells Fargo entered into a conciliation agreement, which required the bank to improve its REO marketing and maintenance practices and to invest $39 million in 45 communities through programs designed to support home ownership, neighborhood stabilization, property rehabilitation, and housing development.[13] In May 2015, NFHA announced that, after a five-year investigation, it had filed with HUD a housing discrimination complaint against Fannie Mae for "wreaking havoc on middle- and working-class communities of color nationwide through a pattern of neglect . . . ."[14]

As of the date of publication, NFHA has filed complaints predicated on similar REO marketing and maintenance claims against Bank of America, Deutsche Bank, and a number of Fannie Mae's service providers.[15]

Furthermore, several municipalities have initiated fair lending lawsuits against mortgage originators and secondary market participants. These cases typically involve allegations that a lender steered minority borrowers into unfavorable or subprime loans, which in turn caused an increase in foreclosures. Other cases involve allegations that lenders failed to adequately provide credit to residents of predominantly minority communities. Due to the resultant rise in foreclosures, municipalities contend that they were economically harmed in several respects, including via lower property values, reduced tax revenues, and the increased demand for health and safety services. Municipalities that have recently filed such lawsuits include Miami and Miami Gardens, Florida; Los Angeles and Oakland, California; and certain counties in both Georgia and Illinois.[16]

While the number of fair lending referrals to DOJ has decreased over the years,[17] the number of public and non-public enforcement actions has been on the rise. This suggests that the agencies with ECOA authority are being more selective about what is referred to DOJ as a "pattern or practice" case (where more than one incident of discrimination is alleged to have occurred),[18] and are instead using their administrative enforcement authority to resolve fair lending issues within the agency. Based on this trend, banks should expect fair lending enforcement to remain active among the DOJ, CFPB, HUD, and prudential regulators.

Risks of Non-Compliance

Under the current regulatory and enforcement environment, violations of the fair lending laws and regulations may result in more frequent examinations, downgrades of a bank's compliance and/or Community Reinvestment Act ratings, and restrictions on a bank's ability to open new branches and engage in mergers or acquisitions, thus potentially prohibiting banks from executing their strategic plans.

Why Every Bank Director Should Read This Handbook

As a member of the board of directors, you are responsible for providing oversight of your bank's fair lending compliance program. In addition to understanding the federal fair lending laws and regulations and recent enforcement trends, regulators will also expect you to be knowledgeable about where fair lending risks exist within your bank. You should understand how and where fair lending risk may arise in your bank's various lending channels and its controls and processes for identifying and addressing fair lending risk. This information should be provided to the board through periodic updates from compliance management and perhaps third-party consultants or legal counsel, depending on the topic.

This Practical Handbook on Fair Lending for Bank Directors and CEOs ("Handbook") is intended to provide members of the American Association of Bank Directors and other bank directors and CEOs with practical tips on how to provide adequate oversight of fair lending risk across their institution. Fair Lending Officers and/or other compliance professionals will also find best practices identified in the Handbook that can be used to enhance their bank's fair lending compliance program.

The Handbook serves as a primer on key federal fair lending laws and highlights recent developments in fair lending enforcement and litigation. The Handbook is not intended to provide legal advice or serve as a comprehensive treatise on fair lending. For fair lending legal advice, we recommend that you consult legal counsel.

Fair lending requirements have evolved from being rules-based — where specific actions are mandated or prohibited — to principles-based, where industry, regulatory, and public interpretations have contributed to setting fair lending compliance expectations and best practices.

As interpreted by the regulators, fair lending obligations are far-reaching and somewhat unpredictable. As a result of these regulatory expectations, fair lending risk management imposes significant compliance burdens upon financial institutions of all sizes. It is important to note, however, that each bank must manage its own fair lending risks; fair lending risk management cannot be outsourced to a third party. Moreover, buyers in the secondary market are not insulated from fair lending risk simply because they did not originate the loan.

Given the government's vigorous supervision and enforcement of fair lending laws and regulations, as well as evolving regulatory expectations, even the most seasoned bank director should read this Handbook (or, at the very least, Chapters I and II with a designated director or member of management reading it in its entirety and reporting to the board). A bank that falls back on yesterday's tried-and-true techniques of managing fair lending risk will fall short of meeting today's regulatory expectations. This new world of fair lending compliance requires bank directors and CEOs to view all aspects of their institution's lending activities through a more critical lens.

CHAPTER II.
YOUR ROLE IN OVERSEEING FAIR LENDING RISK

Regulators expect that a bank's board of directors will play a key role in providing oversight of their institution's fair lending program, which requires hiring competent fair lending risk management staff, providing appropriate resources and budget for the fair lending program, and setting clear expectations concerning the importance of fair lending practices within the bank. This Chapter discusses regulatory expectations for bank directors, and provides guidance on how directors can work to meet those expectations.

A. Board and Management Oversight

To effectively oversee fair lending risk, the board of directors first should be generally knowledgeable about the fair lending laws and regulations. There are two primary federal fair lending laws:

- The **Equal Credit Opportunity Act** ("ECOA") makes it unlawful for any creditor to discriminate against an applicant on a prohibited basis during any aspect of a credit transaction. ECOA applies to both consumer and commercial credit. ECOA also applies to the entire credit life cycle, including product development, advertising, marketing, originations, servicing, collections, and foreclosure or repossession.

- The **Fair Housing Act** ("FHA") makes it unlawful to discriminate in any aspect of the sale, rental, or financing of a dwelling (known as a "residential real estate-related transaction") on a prohibited basis.

There are also several key federal laws that support the objectives of the federal fair lending laws or complement those laws but are not fair lending laws *per se*:

- The **Community Reinvestment Act** ("CRA") was enacted to require banks to provide credit to residents of low- and moderate-income neighborhoods in their local communities, consistent with safe and sound banking practices.

- The **Home Mortgage Disclosure Act** ("HMDA") requires certain mortgage lenders to collect and report to federal regulators, and disclose to the public, certain data about mortgage loan applications and originations, including the race, national origin, and gender of loan applicants.

- Responsible lending laws include Section 5 of the Federal Trade Commission Act ("FTC Act"), which prohibits **unfair or deceptive acts and practices** ("UDAP"), and Sections 1031 and 1036 of the Dodd-Frank Act, which prohibits **unfair, deceptive, or abusive acts or practices** ("UDAAP").

Appendix A contains more detailed information on each of these laws, including a complete listing of the prohibited bases under ECOA and the FHA. Appendix B contains a list of related regulatory guidance and examination procedures.

Typically, a fair lending officer or chief compliance officer is responsible for managing a bank's fair lending program, which includes reporting elevated risks up to management and the board, where appropriate. As a bank director, you are responsible for providing oversight for your bank's fair lending program, together with the rest of the board or a board committee, if authority is delegated to a board committee. Depending on the size of the bank, at least one management-level compliance risk committee may exist to provide more in-depth oversight of the bank's fair lending program. Larger banks may have two or more risk committees that are responsible for managing and addressing fair lending risk.

Both the board of directors (or its delegated committee) and the bank's compliance risk management committee should review and approve the institution's fair lending policy annually, receive copies or summaries of fair lending audit and examination findings, and receive periodic fair lending risk management reports. The latter reports may include fair lending risk assessment results, a report on the state of the fair lending program, statistical analysis results (particularly where disparities are detected and remediation is recommended), and reports on fair lending complaints. Receiving this information on a regular basis will allow the board and any assigned committees to objectively gauge how their bank is managing its fair lending risk and to detect any "red flags" for fair lending risk (discussed further in Chapter V).

Reports should be appropriately calibrated so that the board of directors receives the most critical information that it needs to know in a form that is meaningful and clear, whereas compliance risk management committees should receive more in-depth reports that allow the committee to review more detailed information and data.

Regulators frequently evaluate board and board committee minutes to ensure that directors are actively engaged in fair lending oversight. Therefore, board and board committee minutes should reflect any dialogue at the meetings about reports included in the board or board committee packet.

B. Asking the Right Questions

To understand your bank's fair lending risks and controls, you should review the results from your bank's fair lending risk assessment. Regulators typically expect such risk assessments to be performed annually.

To fully appreciate a bank's fair lending risk, it is important for directors to ask the right questions when engaging in a dialogue with compliance and legal staff. Below are some common questions that may be appropriate for you to ask to assess your bank's fair lending risk:

Questions for Bank Directors to Assess Fair Lending Risk

- Where do the greatest fair lending risks lie within our bank?

- What controls do we have in place to manage those risks?

    o Are those controls formalized in policies and procedures or more of a business practice?

    o Are those controls automated or manual?

    o Are those controls tested periodically to ensure that they are working properly? If so, what are the results of those tests? Who receives the results from that testing within our bank?

- To what degree does our bank allow the use of discretion by underwriters, loan officers, or third parties (*e.g.*, mortgage brokers or auto dealers) in underwriting or pricing?

- How does our bank manage credit or pricing exceptions?

    o Does our bank limit those exceptions to a certain percentage of loan volume (*e.g.*, 10 to 20%)?

    o Are exception reports generated and are they reviewed by compliance for potential fair lending risk?

- How does our bank evaluate fair lending risk for new or modified loan products and policies?

- What processes and controls does the bank employ concerning third parties' originating loans for the bank?

- Has our bank evaluated fair lending risk in loan servicing activities (known as "fair servicing risk")?

  - What controls does the bank have in place to ensure that consistent levels of service are provided to customers?

- Have there been any recent examinations or compliance department or audit findings concerning our bank's non-compliance with fair lending laws and regulations?

- What are some best practices that our bank's peers are doing to manage their fair lending risk that our bank is not doing?

- Has our bank received any consumer complaints alleging discrimination or unfair treatment?

  - If so, do the complaints reveal any trends?

  - Have any complaints led to litigation or regulatory involvement?

- What do you believe are emerging fair lending issues that our bank should be concerned about?

These types of questions will demonstrate to management and regulators that you understand the importance of controlling the bank's fair lending risk and help establish a culture of compliance in this critical area.

C. Hiring or Developing a Fair Lending Officer

In today's regulatory environment, banks should strongly consider having a fair lending officer on staff to manage the bank's fair lending program, work with the business unit management to identify and address fair lending risks, and interface with regulators. Depending on the size, scope, and complexity of your bank's products/services and its geographic lending footprint, you may not have a dedicated fair lending officer. Instead, a compliance officer may wear more than one hat and manage compliance for multiple areas.

Although the ideal fair lending officer candidate should already have fair lending compliance risk management experience, fair lending officers are in high demand by banks and even non-banks subject to fair lending laws. As a result, qualified candidates are often difficult to find and recruit. Therefore, some banks may need to consider developing an internal or external candidate with some compliance experience through mentoring.

If seeking a qualified candidate externally, it may be a good idea to hire a professional search firm that specializes in finding compliance professionals across the U.S. Ideally, fair lending officer candidates should have an undergraduate degree, at least five years of experience in compliance risk management, prior experience as a fair lending officer, and experience in interacting with, and making presentations to, executive management and regulators.

While it is preferable to look for a candidate who already has fair lending compliance risk management experience, if an individual has a fairly extensive background in compliance generally, he or she could likely transition into a role as a fair lending officer with adequate guidance and mentoring. It may be appropriate to start a less seasoned fair lending professional as a fair lending manager until they develop more expertise in the area.

If a qualified external candidate cannot be found, then one option is to develop an internal candidate. Banks often take one of two approaches: (i) developing a candidate who is already a member of the compliance risk management group (usually a compliance manager), or (ii) grooming a business manager who has extensive knowledge of lending products and/or underwriting and pricing practices.

Development of either an external or internal candidate may take place by having the chief compliance officer and/or in-house fair lending attorney (or outside counsel) mentor the individual and teach him or her fair lending concepts and risks. The individual should learn the business on an in-depth basis — particularly underwriting, pricing, and loss mitigation practices — for both mortgage and non-mortgage products.

Sometimes when neither an appropriate internal nor external candidate can be found to assume the role of fair lending officer, a bank may choose to table the search for a period of time and instead engage an experienced compliance consultant to serve as the fair lending officer on a temporary basis (*e.g.*, 3 to 6 months). Although this approach can be costly, it addresses the need to fill the role while moving the fair lending program forward until the right candidate can be found.

D. Fair Lending Program Resources

Once a fair lending officer is in place, it will be critical to ensure that he or she has an appropriate team, tools, budget, and resources to support the program. Regulators expect that the board of directors will ensure that appropriate staffing and resources are provided for the fair lending program, which should be commensurate with the size, complexity, and risk profile of the institution. Periodically, fair lending program resources should be revisited to ensure that they continue to meet the institution's needs.

E. Integration of Responsible Lending Concepts into Fair Lending Programs

In recent years, many financial institutions have expanded their existing fair lending programs by incorporating responsible lending concepts to reflect an increasing emphasis by regulators, the media, consumer advocacy groups, and consumers themselves on responsible lending practices. Responsible lending requires compliance with several laws, including UDAAP, and focuses on equitable treatment of, and transparency toward, consumers by providing full disclosure and informed choice to consumers.

Responsible lending is viewed as a concept that is highly complementary to fair lending, so regulators view combined fair and responsible lending programs favorably.

In light of these developments and as you oversee your bank's fair lending program in your role as a bank director, you should consider whether it may be appropriate to expand the scope of your institution's program to include responsible lending concepts to keep pace with regulatory expectations.

CHAPTER III.
WHAT TYPES OF LENDING DISCRIMINATION VIOLATE THE FAIR LENDING LAWS?

Courts have recognized three legal theories under which government agencies and plaintiffs may bring cases alleging discrimination.

A. Overt Discrimination

Overt discrimination occurs when a lender openly discriminates against an applicant or a borrower on a prohibited basis. Overt discrimination may include written policies or procedures. For example, if a lender has a policy where it offers a credit card with a limit of up to $750 for applicants aged 21 to 30 and $1,500 for applicants over 30, this policy would likely be viewed as discriminatory based on age. Overt discrimination may also include oral statements where a lender expresses a discriminatory preference, even if the lender does not act upon this preference. For instance, overt discrimination on the basis of gender occurs if a lender states that it prefers not to make loans to women. In the fair lending arena, overt discrimination is relatively uncommon.

B. Disparate Treatment

Disparate treatment occurs when a lender intentionally treats an applicant or a borrower differently on a prohibited basis. This standard does not require any evidence that the treatment was motivated by prejudice or that the lender intended to discriminate against a particular class of persons. Disparate treatment can occur simply by treating similarly situated people differently on a prohibited basis without a legitimate, nondiscriminatory reason for that difference in treatment.

To illustrate, disparate treatment occurs when a loan officer processes loan applications for non-minority applicants immediately, but informs minority loan applicants that it would take several days to process an application. The most common disparate treatment cases arise from allegations of pricing or denial disparities that are unfavorable to borrowers in a prohibited basis group.

C. Disparate Impact

Disparate impact occurs when a lender applies a facially neutral policy or a practice equally to all applicants or borrowers, but the policy or practice has a disproportionately negative effect on members of a protected class. To prove disparate impact, there is no need to demonstrate that the bank intended to discriminate.

For example, the regulators take the position that a policy establishing a minimum loan amount for single family home mortgages may disproportionately affect minority purchasers, who may have lower incomes or wish to buy homes in areas with lower property values, thus resulting in disparate impact.[19] Under the disparate impact theory of discrimination, the plaintiff is not required to establish intent and, therefore, it is irrelevant whether the bank actually intended to discriminate on a prohibited basis. Courts have traditionally applied a three-step, burden-shifting test to determine whether a defendant can be found liable under the fair lending laws for discrimination under a disparate impact test.

First, the plaintiff must allege that the lender's neutral policy or practice, when applied equally to all credit applicants, disproportionately excludes or burdens a protected class of applicants on a prohibited basis, resulting in disparate impact. Second, the lender must refute this allegation by demonstrating that the policy or practice is justified by business necessity. This is often known as "business justification," and relevant factors may include cost, competition, and profitability, among others. In the third step, even if the lender can show a business justification or necessity, the practice may still be found to be in violation if an alternative policy/practice could serve the same purpose with less discriminatory effect.

In February 2013, HUD issued a final rule that codifies its standards for disparate impact claims brought under the FHA. Under this rule, once a lender's practice has been shown by the plaintiff to have a disparate impact on a protected class, the lender would then have the burden of showing that the challenged practice "is necessary to achieve one or more of its substantial, legitimate, nondiscriminatory interests."[20] This second step is different than the traditional test used by courts, as explained above. Even if the lender can satisfy this burden, under the rule, courts can find that the lender violated the FHA if another practice could serve the same purpose with less discriminatory effect. Because HUD's burden-shifting standard differs from the standard articulated in case law, it is unclear how the courts will interpret this rule.[21]

In a narrow 5-4 vote in *Texas Department of Housing and Community Affairs v. Inclusive Communities Project,*[22] the U.S. Supreme Court concluded that Congress intended the FHA to permit disparate impact claims based on its interpretation of the FHA's text, the amendment history of the FHA, and the purpose of the FHA. Therefore, the Court held that a defendant may be liable under the FHA for a policy or practice that has an adverse impact on members of a particular protected class group.

The Court did not address HUD's disparate impact rule in its opinion, but Court instead focused on the three-step, burden-shifting framework used by the courts to prove disparate impact claims by clarifying its interpretation of that framework.[23]

While the burden-shifting framework described by the Supreme Court appears to be different than the version of the burden-shifting test contained in HUD's disparate impact rule, it remains to be seen how the Supreme Court's decision will be applied by lower courts going forward.

The Supreme Court's decision in *Inclusive Communities* is expected to embolden government agencies and private plaintiffs to continue to assert claims of disparate impact discrimination under the FHA and ECOA. Therefore, it is advisable for banks to examine new and existing policies, procedures, and business practices for the potential risk of disparate impact and take steps to reduce fair lending risk. This may include modifying or discontinuing the policy or practice, or reaching a satisfactory conclusion that the policy/practice does not in fact cause disparate impact by using the Supreme Court's approach to the three-step test.

D. Redlining, Reverse Redlining, and Steering

Within the three theories of fair lending claims (overt discrimination, disparate treatment, and disparate impact), there are different types of lending discrimination that can be raised by a regulator or plaintiff. Examples include allegations of redlining, reverse redlining and steering.

What Is Redlining?

Redlining occurs when a bank refuses to extend credit or provides unequal access to credit in certain neighborhoods because of the race, ethnicity, national origin, or other protected characteristic of its residents. There has been a steady stream of redlining cases brought by DOJ since 1994, most of which have been brought against smaller banks. Two examples are discussed below.

Examples: Redlining Enforcement Actions – Small Banks Are Not Safe

In January 2013, DOJ entered into a $165,000 settlement with Community State Bank to resolve allegations that the Michigan community bank served the credit needs of white neighborhoods in the Saginaw and Flint metropolitan areas to a significantly greater extent than it served the credit needs of majority African American neighborhoods.[24]

In June 2011, DOJ entered into a $3.6 million settlement with Citizens Republic Bancorp, Inc. ("Citizens") to resolve allegations that Citizens "engaged in a race-based pattern of locating or acquiring branch offices" to serve the credit needs of white neighborhoods in Detroit to a greater extent than majority African American neighborhoods.[25]

Also in June 2011, DOJ entered into a settlement with Midwest BankCentre for $1.45 million to resolve allegations that the bank served the credit needs of residents of predominantly white neighborhoods in the St. Louis metropolitan area to a greater extent than it served the credit needs of majority African American neighborhoods.[26]

Traditionally, regulators have evaluated redlining risk by reviewing a bank's CRA assessment area. Heightened redlining risk was indicated if a bank's main office and/or branches operated in or around historically racially segregated cities or if a bank chose to close a branch in an area with a high proportion of minority residents without reasonable business justification. Although banks should continue to ensure that their CRA assessment areas do not exclude any geographic areas with higher concentrations of minority residents and evaluate their branch opening/closing strategy in such areas, regulators are defining redlining risk quite differently in recent years. Importantly, a bank's various entry points into the market must demonstrate diversity. Some of the new triggers for redlining risk include the following:

- Lack of marketing and advertising in minority media
- Lack of products that tend to be more appealing to residents of census tracts with a majority of minorities (known as "majority-minority" census tracts)
- Geographic placement of loan officers in primarily non-minority census tract locations
- Geographic placement of third-party loan referral sources, such as brokers and real estate agents
- Lack of loan officers focused on CRA lending

Regulators are also looking at applying disparate impact theories in redlining allegations — in particular, whether a bank's policies or procedures may cause a disparate impact of not lending to minorities in certain geographic areas.

As noted in the list of redlining risk triggers above, regulators are now extending redlining risk to lenders that engage only in wholesale lending. Increasingly, there appears to be aregulatory expectation that such lenders will seek out brokers to penetrate majority-minority census tracts by obtaining loans from minority borrowers and that wholesale lenders will make other affirmative efforts to penetrate those markets. Over time, this expectation may extend to auto dealers.

Example: Redlining Enforcement Actions – An Area of Focus for State Regulators

In September 2014, the New York Attorney General ("NYAG") sued a regional bank alleging that the bank failed to offer mortgage products to residents of predominantly African American neighborhoods in Buffalo, New York.[27] In the press release announcing the lawsuit, the NYAG stated that this case was part of ongoing investigations by the NYAG into potential redlining activities across the state.[28]

What Is Reverse Redlining?

Reverse redlining occurs when a bank intentionally targets the marketing of certain products or services with less favorable terms, conditions, and/or pricing toward a particular group on a prohibited basis, such as race, ethnicity, or national origin. In recent years, several municipalities filed cases against residential mortgage lenders based on reverse redlining allegations that they targeted minority communities for subprime loans, and that defaults on those loans led to foreclosures and vacancies, which in turn resulted in increased municipal costs and decreased property tax revenues.[29]

Examples: Reverse Redlining Enforcement Actions

In February 2015, DOJ, together with the U.S. Attorney's Office for the Western District of North Carolina and the North Carolina Department of Justice, announced a settlement of DOJ's first discrimination lawsuit involving "buy here, pay here" auto lending.[30] The $225,000 settlement resolved allegations that two North Carolina-based used car dealerships, among other things, engaged in reverse redlining by intentionally targeting African-American customers for predatory car loans. The settlement requires substantial reforms to the dealerships' lending and servicing practices.

What Is Steering?

Steering involves promoting different programs within a loan type (*e.g.*, prime versus subprime auto loans) with less favorable terms, conditions, or pricing to otherwise qualified borrowers in a way that treats them differently on a prohibited basis.

Example: Steering Lawsuit

In February 2015, the Fair Housing Justice Center, a New York City-based fair housing non-profit organization, filed a lawsuit against one of the top 20 largest banks in the U.S. alleging that the bank's loan officers in New York City (i) used neighborhood racial demographics to steer minorities to racially segregated neighborhoods and (ii) steered prospective buyers to mortgage loan products with different terms and conditions based on race and national origin.[31] The organization hired nine female "testers" of varying racial and ethnic backgrounds who acted as first-time homebuyers who were married and without children. The organization alleged that the bank's loan officers encouraged minority testers to apply for loan programs that were limited to homes located in [majority-minority] neighborhoods or in low-to-moderate income areas, and discouraged white testers from doing so. The organization also alleged that the bank favored white applicants during the prequalification process. For instance, it was alleged that a more qualified Hispanic tester was told that she would qualify for a mortgage $125,000 less than what a white tester could obtain.

CHAPTER IV.
WHERE DOES FAIR LENDING RISK LIE?

Although regulators have traditionally focused on lending areas that permit human judgment (*e.g.*, underwriting and pricing), fair lending requirements apply to all aspects of credit-related lending and servicing activities, which include:

- New product development
- Advertising and marketing
- Taking and processing applications
- Pricing
- Credit risk and underwriting
- Account servicing activities
- Collections
- Loss mitigation and loan modifications
- Repossession and foreclosure
- REO property maintenance

Fair lending obligations apply to all consumer and commercial credit products, including but not limited to mortgage loans, auto loans, unsecured loans, credit cards, student loans, overdraft protection and small business loans. This Chapter discusses some of the key sources of risk in the credit administration process and product-specific considerations.

It's important to note that fair lending risk may arise well before a prospective customer actually applies for credit. In particular, fair lending implications should be considered when developing strategies regarding where a bank will establish branches, which products it will develop or offer, and to whom the bank will target in its product advertising and marketing efforts. As a bank director, you will want to ask whether your bank's branching, new product development, or marketing strategies may create possible redlining, reverse redlining, or steering risk.

A. New Product Development

It is critical to ensure that any new lending products or services are developed, implemented, and maintained in a manner that complies with fair and responsible lending laws. To that end, it is important that legal and compliance representatives have a seat at the table as new products or services are being discussed and designed, and then are part of the review and approval process as new products and/or services are implemented.

Although the board of directors has responsibility for product development oversight, the new product and service review and approval process is typically executed through a new product development committee or managed through an appropriate compliance risk management committee that includes representatives from legal and compliance on the committee. Alternatively, it may involve *ad hoc*, product-specific meetings with written sign-off required on the new initiative by legal and/or compliance representatives. Regardless of the internal process chosen, it is imperative to demonstrate that compliance with fair lending laws was considered and addressed as part of the new product and service development and implementation process.

B. Advertising and Marketing

The two federal fair lending laws — ECOA and the FHA — each contain provisions related to non-discriminatory advertising for extensions of credit. Banks may not directly or indirectly engage in any marketing or advertising that would discourage or selectively encourage, on a prohibited basis, a reasonable person from making or pursuing an application for credit. Specifically, a bank cannot either expressly state or imply a preference for, or exclusion of, any customers on a prohibited basis. Under the fair lending laws, banks must also ensure that any marketing response models or other methods used to identify or select the recipients of advertising or promotional materials comply with applicable fair and responsible lending laws.

Where required, advertising and marketing materials in connection with mortgage lending activities must include a facsimile of the equal housing opportunity logo and the phrase "Equal Opportunity Lender" or a statement to the effect that the bank makes housing loans without regard to an applicant's prohibited basis characteristics.

As a best practice, it is a good idea to require preapproval from legal and/or compliance prior to using any advertising or marketing materials. This approach helps ensure that any advertising and marketing materials comply with applicable laws, including the fair lending laws. Compliance with responsible lending laws such as UDAAP should also be considered as part of the review by legal and compliance of any advertising and marketing materials.

Example: Redlining Enforcement Actions – Marketing Models Matter

In June 2014, the CFPB and DOJ announced parallel enforcement actions — totaling $169 million — against Synchrony Bank, formerly known as GE Capital Retail Bank, based on allegations that the bank excluded borrowers from credit card repayment programs who indicated that they preferred communications to be in Spanish or who had a mailing address in Puerto Rico, even if the customers met the promotion's qualifications. The CFPB and DOJ asserted that as a result, Hispanic populations were unfairly denied the opportunity to benefit from certain promotions.[32] The Synchrony Bank settlement reinforces the importance of considering fair lending implications in all aspects of a bank's marketing activities.

C. Loan Origination

1. Mortgage Lending

Regulatory enforcement actions involving mortgage lending continue to concentrate on the use of loan officer and broker discretion in pricing. Even pricing disparities of less than 10 basis points are now enough to result in a referral to DOJ. Enforcement actions also continue to focus on judgmental underwriting practices, with federal agencies' renewed emphasis on access to credit following the financial crisis.

Pricing disparities are also not restricted to the overall annual percentage rate and may focus on an isolated disparity in fees, even if there is no allegation that the overall cost of the loan was higher.[33] For example, DOJ entered into a $6.1 million settlement with AIG Federal Savings Bank in 2010 to resolve allegations that it allowed wholesale mortgage brokers to charge African American borrowers higher upfront broker fees than to white borrowers from 2003 to 2006.

More Examples: Discretionary Pricing

In December 2013, DOJ and the CFPB entered into a $35 million settlement with PNC Bank, as successor-in-interest to National City Bank, to resolve discriminatory pricing allegations.[34] The allegations were based on pricing disparities for African American and Hispanic borrowers as low as nine basis points. In 2013, DOJ also entered into settlements based on discriminatory pricing allegations with Chevy Chase Bank and Southport Bank, which required consumer restitution of $2.85 million and $687,000, respectively.[35]

Regulators have also sharpened their focus on the lending practices of certain mortgage lenders to determine if they had illegally denied any applicants' mortgages, or refinancings of mortgages, based on sex, familial status, or disability because the woman was pregnant or on maternity leave. Beginning in June 2010, the U.S. Department of Housing and Urban Development ("HUD") launched several investigations, and in July 2010, HUD began issuing a series of enforcement actions against mortgage lenders and mortgage insurers alleging discrimination against pregnant women or those on maternity leave.

Example: Maternity Leave Discrimination

On July 1, 2014, HUD announced a conciliation agreement with Greenlight Financial Services ("Greenlight") to resolve allegations that it violated the FHA when it denied or delayed processing of mortgage loans to women because they were on maternity leave.[36] The conciliation agreement was driven by a complaint from a married couple alleging that Greenlight denied their refinancing application because the wife was on maternity leave. HUD's investigation revealed that Greenlight also allegedly denied four other applicants who were on maternity leave, or delayed their applications until after the women returned to work. The agreement required that Greenlight pay $20,000 to the couple who filed the complaint, and $7,000 to each of the other four applicants identified by HUD.

a. Fair Lending and the Qualified Mortgage Rule

In recent years, lenders have expressed concern that the CFPB's Ability-to-Repay/Qualified Mortgage Rule would increase their exposure to fair lending risk. This concern arises from the fact that a choice to make only qualified mortgages would effectively exclude consumers with debt-to-income ratios above 43% and/or consumers who cannot qualify for loans under the standards for loans eligible for guarantee, insurance, or purchase by the federal agencies or Fannie Mae and Freddie Mac.

On October 22, 2013, the CFPB, OCC, Federal Deposit Insurance Corporation ("FDIC"), Board of Governors of the Federal Reserve System ("FRB"), and the National Credit Union Administration ("NCUA") (collectively, the "authoring agencies") issued a joint statement ("2013 Interagency Statement") in response to inquiries from creditors concerning their liability under ECOA by originating only qualified mortgages.[37] Notably, DOJ and HUD did not participate in the 2013 Interagency Statement. The 2013 Interagency Statement does not state that a creditor's choice to limit its offerings to qualified mortgages or safe harbor qualified mortgages would comply with ECOA; rather, the authoring agencies state that they "do not anticipate that a creditor's decision to offer only qualified mortgages would, absent other factors, elevate a supervised institution's fair lending risk."[38]

2. Auto Lending

Indirect auto lending has been an increasing area of focus for the regulators. In the CFPB's Fair Lending Report to Congress issued in April 2015, it announced, for the second consecutive year, that auto finance would be a key priority for the agency's fair lending supervisory and enforcement work.[39] In September 2014, the CFPB released additional guidance on its plans to supervise and enforce auto finance companies' compliance with consumer finance laws, including fair lending laws.[40]

In 2013, the CFPB issued a bulletin that provides general guidance with respect to fair lending compliance and the indirect auto lending industry.[41] In that bulletin, the CFPB contends that by permitting dealer mark-up and compensating dealers on that discretionary basis, lenders may be liable under the legal theories of both disparate treatment and disparate impact when pricing disparities on prohibited bases exist within their portfolios.[42] The CFPB has taken the position that dealer mark-up and compensation policies are alone sufficient to trigger lender liability. The CFPB has also suggested that lenders should either eliminate dealer pricing discretion or be required to establish a comprehensive fair lending program to mitigate the risk of discretionary dealer mark-up.

In December 2013, the CFPB and DOJ announced their first joint fair lending enforcement action against an indirect auto finance company to resolve allegations that Ally Bank's and Ally Financial's dealer compensation policy, which allowed for auto dealer discretion in pricing, resulted in a disparate impact on certain minority borrowers.[43] The $98 million settlement is DOJ's third largest fair lending enforcement action ever.

In May 2015, DOJ announced its settlement with Evergreen Bank Group, a small state-chartered bank regulated by the FDIC at the federal level, to resolve allegations involving discriminatory motorcycle lending through the bank's FreedomRoad Financial lending unit. Under the terms of the settlement, the bank was required to reduce or eliminate the level of discretion granted to dealers in pricing motorcycle loans and pay $395,000 in customer remediation to 2,200 borrowers.[44] Evergreen Bank Group agreed to adopt a policy eliminating dealer discretion to increase interest rates and instead now compensates dealers based on a percentage of the principal amount of the loan that does not vary based on the loan's interest rate.

With the CFPB's guidance on indirect auto lending and the Ally Bank settlement, indirect auto lenders are on notice of the regulatory expectation to impose sufficient controls or revise dealer mark-up and compensation policies, implement a strong fair lending compliance and monitoring program, and address risks through monitoring and corrective action programs.

3. Unsecured Lending

Since 2011, the CFPB has been gathering information on payday and other short-term lending products. The CFPB has expressed concerns that short-term loans are "debt traps" and cautioned that the agency is "determining how to exercise [its] authorities to best protect consumers while preserving access to responsible credit."[45]

Prudential regulators, namely the FDIC and the FRB, have referred matters involving unsecured consumer loans to DOJ during this same time frame.

Examples: Unsecured Lending Enforcement Actions Originated by the Prudential Regulators

DOJ's settlement with Nixon State Bank in 2011 marked the agency's first pricing discrimination lawsuit involving unsecured consumer loans in more than 10 years.[46] Under the terms of that settlement, the bank was required to pay nearly $100,000, conduct employee training, and revise pricing policies that were alleged to have resulted in higher prices on unsecured loans made to Hispanic borrowers in violation of ECOA.

In 2013, DOJ announced its $159,000 settlement with Fort Davis State Bank, which was also based on claims that the bank charged higher prices for unsecured consumer loans to Hispanic borrowers in a discriminatory manner.[47] *Nixon* and *Fort Davis State Bank* arose from examinations conducted by the FDIC in 2010 and 2011, respectively. For both cases, it is noteworthy that DOJ claimed that loan officers were given broad discretion in the origination and pricing process, which in turn led to a disparate impact on Hispanic borrowers. More recently, in January 2015, DOJ announced a $140,000 settlement with First United Bank, predicated on similar claims. *First United Bank* was also referred to DOJ by the FDIC.[48]

Fair lending risk in unsecured lending may arise in several contexts, including marketing, origination, product usage, payment processing, collection practices, and third-party relationships.

Marketing materials and sales tactics should be evaluated to ensure that payday and other short-term lending products are not being targeted to protected class borrowers. Although race and ethnicity data are limited for non-mortgage credit, some studies have suggested that protected classes comprise a larger percentage of the payday loan borrower population. For example, a consumer group study reported that over one-quarter of all bank payday borrowers are Social Security recipients.[49]

4. Credit Cards

Regulators have identified several areas of fair lending risk when offering credit cards — from marketing strategies to underwriting and ancillary products to rewards programs for high-net worth clientele.

Fair lending risk in credit card extensions of credit has been an area of focus for the FRB in recent years. In August 2014, the Federal Reserve Bank of Philadelphia released a discussion paper titled "Fair Lending Analysis of Credit Cards,"[50] which addresses fair lending risks in various stages of the marketing, acquisition, and management of credit card accounts.

One month later, an FRB economist published an article titled, "Race, Ethnicity, and Credit Card Marketing,"[51] which examines the relationship between race, ethnicity, and the probability that a borrower would receive a credit card offer — via a direct mail solicitation — from one of five top credit card issuers. The article reported that even after controlling for credit history, household income, and local economic conditions, Black borrowers were 27% less likely to receive a credit card offer, and Hispanic borrowers were 17% less likely to receive a credit card offer. The article underscores the importance of marketing in providing equal access to credit and calls on the CFPB to conduct further investigation.

As with other lending channels, a bank should review underwriting and pricing practices (including scorecards, pricing exceptions, and credit policy overrides) for fair lending compliance. Credit line increases and decreases should also be conducted in a fair and consistent manner. Advertising and marketing strategies and materials must be reviewed for fair lending compliance and appropriately reflect diversity.

Regulators have become increasingly concerned with a credit card provider's target or suppression marketing criteria. Banks should closely review marketing campaigns that exclude certain marketing segments to ensure that these exclusions are not based on protected class characteristics. Many credit card providers offer special benefits, terms, or products to its premier or high-net worth customers. These programs and products in particular should be reviewed for potential fair lending risk. It is also important to ensure that clear, consistent, and nondiscriminatory criteria for your bank's programs and products are well documented.

5. Student Lending

Student loans have surpassed credit cards as the largest source of unsecured consumer debt. As a result, the CFPB has made student lending a priority and has taken several steps to implement and expand its oversight of student lenders.

Credit and pricing models that use non-credit bureau attributes are particularly susceptible to regulatory scrutiny. These attributes include cohort default rates, graduation rates, retention rates, and whether a school is a for-profit/not-for-profit or a two-year/four-year institution. For example, the CFPB's examination guidelines require that examiners determine whether the lender uses cohort default rates ("CDRs") and evaluate the entity's justification for using this attribute.[52] CDRs are a measure of the federal student loan repayment history of a particular group or "cohort" of borrowers. CDR is often used by private student lenders as a proxy for a student's likelihood of repaying debt as part of underwriting and pricing decisions. This can pose fair lending concerns because racial and ethnic minority students are disproportionately concentrated in schools with higher CDRs.

A regulator may also scrutinize a bank's assessment of a student's future ability to pay. Typically, an ability-to-pay analysis in the student loan context is based on a student's major or future occupation, which may present fair lending concerns, particularly under the disparate impact theory. This is because certain protected classes may be over represented in certain occupations. Teaching and nursing are two examples of traditionally female-dominated professions.

As with other credit products, marketing practices are also a key focal point for the regulators. The CFPB has examined how student borrowers are solicited and whether the lender has used different marketing efforts based on loan product (*e.g.*, products for certain majors), schools, or geography.[53] In the servicing context, lenders should also ensure that borrowers are treated fairly and consistently in loan modifications, collections, and fee waivers.

6. Overdraft

Although regulatory compliance concerns for overdraft programs primarily involve UDAP or UDAAP issues — such as re-ordering checking account transactions in a manner that increases consumer cost, missing or confusing information, misleading marketing materials, and disproportionate impact on low-income and younger consumers — overdraft programs are also subject to ECOA.

In 2005, the OCC, FRB, FDIC, and NCUA issued joint guidance on overdraft protection programs. In that guidance, the agencies stated that "steering or targeting certain consumers on a prohibited basis for overdraft protection programs while offering other consumers overdraft lines of credit or other more favorable credit products or overdraft services, will raise concerns under the ECOA."[54]

In addition, the FDIC has issued guidance to clarify that a bank's "[i]nconsistent application of waivers of overdraft fees will be evaluated in light of fair lending statutes and regulations."[55] Therefore, it is important to review your institution's overdraft program for both responsible lending (UDAP/UDAAP) and fair lending concerns.

D. Servicing, Loss Mitigation, and REO

Since the mortgage crisis in 2008, regulators have expected that financial institutions will engage in "fair servicing" activities by treating borrowers fairly, consistently, and objectively in the servicing, collections, loss mitigation, and foreclosure processes. Banks should develop controls to ensure the fair and consistent treatment of customers in credit line increases and decreases, account closures, fee waivers, collections, loss mitigation, and foreclosure.

Fair servicing issues arise most often in the context of delinquent and defaulted loans. For instance, the U.S. Treasury Department requires the collection of demographic data (including race and ethnicity) on borrowers who apply for loans under the Home Affordable Modification Program ("HAMP"), in addition to information about loan modification requests, and the outcome of the modification. Borrowers should see parity in lender outreach and should receive uniform information relating to loss mitigation.

As discussed in the Introduction, the NFHA has initiated several lawsuits against banks, servicers, and third-party vendors involving claims that REO properties in minority communities were not maintained and marketed in the same manner as REO properties in majority white communities. The first of these lawsuits, which involved Wells Fargo, settled in June 2013.[56] The NFHA and HUD also initiated a lawsuit against Fannie Mae, one the nation's largest owners of foreclosed properties, based on similar claims.[57] The FRB identified disparate treatment of REO properties as a "hot topic" in its October 2014 Outlook Live series webinar.

CHAPTER V.
SPOTTING "RED FLAGS" FOR FAIR LENDING RISK

This Chapter identifies six common "red flags" for fair lending risk that you should be aware of so you can determine whether your bank is taking appropriate steps to identify, manage, and mitigate those risks.[58] As a bank director, it is important for you to keep a watchful eye out for these and other red flags as you review your bank's compliance reports and engage in discussions with your bank's legal and compliance staff. Examples of other red flags are found in endnote 59.

Red Flag #1: Use of discretion in consumer lending.

As we discussed in Chapter III, areas that allow discretion in the lending process attract regulatory scrutiny and increase fair lending risk. Specifically, policies and procedures often permit loan officers, underwriters, or third parties (*e.g.*, mortgage brokers or auto dealers) to exercise discretion in underwriting and pricing. Discretionary practices may also arise in account maintenance (*e.g.*, fee waivers), collections, and loss mitigation.

If your bank allows for discretion in the loan origination or servicing process, it is important to ensure that appropriate controls are in place and to perform ongoing monitoring and testing of the discretionary activity. Controls, monitoring, and testing help ensure that discretion is exercised consistently; if not, appropriate remedial action can then be taken so that the consumer is not harmed.

Red Flag #2: Lack of periodic fair lending risk assessments.

As discussed further in Chapter V, regulators expect that banks of all sizes will conduct periodic fair lending risk assessments of its products, services, delivery channels, and operations to evaluate its level of compliance with applicable laws and regulations. Not conducting such risk assessments may cause the regulators to do a more in-depth assessment during examinations and raise questions about a bank's commitment to consumer compliance.

Fair lending risk assessments may be conducted based on your bank's qualitative measures, quantitative analysis, or a combination of both. The methodology for the risk assessment should be reviewed periodically to reflect changes to applicable laws and regulations, and your own bank's products, services or business practices. The results of the risk assessments should be used to ensure that proper controls are in place at your bank (especially for high-risk areas) and to help allocate your compliance staff, budget, and resources.

Red Flag #3: Disparate impact that may not be readily apparent.

Potential disparate impact is often difficult to detect, so it is important to proactively review your bank's policies, practices, and procedures to determine if a risk of disparate impact may exist. This may be done through statistical analyses and other quantitative or qualitative reviews.

Chapter VIII discusses the types of statistical analyses that a bank could perform to assess its level of fair lending risk.

Your bank should review marketing, advertising, underwriting, pricing, compensation, and other related policies and procedures to evaluate whether they could have a disproportionately adverse impact on a protected class. If there is a potential disparate impact, your bank should determine whether the level of risk merits performing a formal, documented disparate impact analysis. This would include a determination of whether an adequate business justification for the policy or procedure exists, and whether there is a less discriminatory alternative that could achieve the same results.

Red Flag #4: Failure to evaluate fair lending risks and controls for non-mortgage loans.

For non-mortgage loan products, the government has relied on proxy data to conduct quantitative analyses in the absence of any HMDA data to serve as the basis of a fair lending claim. For example, in 2014, the CFPB issued a white paper on the proxy methodology it uses to analyze fair lending compliance for auto loans.[59] Depending on the level of risk and availability of suitable proxy data, your bank can determine whether it is appropriate to perform some preliminary testing on non-mortgage products. At a minimum, all banks should review their preventive and detective controls for their non-mortgage lending channels to determine whether proper controls are in place.

Red Flag #5: Lending policies that require a minimum loan amount.

Underwriting guidelines that impose minimum loan amounts have been the subject of numerous fair lending complaints and settlements. This is due to the perception that minimum loan amounts have a disparate impact on minority borrowers who are more likely to live in neighborhoods and communities with lower property values and, therefore, require lower loan amounts.

As a case in point, on September 12, 2012, DOJ announced into a $2 million settlement with Luther Burbank Savings for setting a minimum loan amount of $400,000 for its wholesale single-family residential mortgage lending program.[60] DOJ alleged that this policy resulted in very few mortgage loan originations to African American or Hispanic borrowers.

This principle applies to both mortgage and non-mortgage products, especially to the extent that the minimum loan amount makes a product inaccessible to members of a protected class. To understand your bank's fair lending risk in this area, legal and compliance staff should review your bank's lending policies and procedures to identify any minimum loan amounts.

Red Flag #6: Credit overlays to underwriting guidelines.

Your bank should regularly monitor whether certain credit overlays to underwriting guidelines have a disproportionate adverse effect on members of a protected class. Some examples of credit overlays that should be monitored on a regular basis include: (a) higher minimum FICO scores for Federal Housing Administration loans than what is required by HUD; (b) requiring female applicants on maternity leave to return to work before closing a mortgage loan (even when the applicant satisfies the income requirements while she is on maternity leave); and (c) requiring applicants receiving permanent disability benefits from the Social Security Administration to provide proof of continuation of the disability with a letter from a physician attesting to the nature of the disability and the expected duration of the disability.

CHAPTER IV.
FAIR LENDING RISK MANAGEMENT – HOW STRONG IS YOUR BANK'S PROGRAM?

In designing or evaluating your bank's fair lending program, it is important to recognize that there is no "one size fits all" approach. Each bank must develop and implement its own fair lending program that is tailored to the bank's size, complexity, and risk profile. Your bank should also strongly consider incorporating responsible lending concepts into its fair lending risk management program to manage fair and responsible lending risks, including UDAP and UDAAP. This Chapter provides an overview of the key components of an effective fair lending compliance program.

A. A Fair Lending Policy Is Critical

A comprehensive, enterprise-wide fair lending policy is key to establishing a corporate culture that is focused on the fair and equitable treatment of consumers throughout the product life cycle. A fair lending policy that is reviewed and approved by the board of directors at least annually can demonstrate a bank's commitment to providing a "top down" approach to managing fair lending risk that starts with sound board and management oversight. A fair lending policy also serves to form the framework of your bank's fair lending program.

B. Fair Lending Program Elements

1. Risk Assessment

A fair lending risk assessment should be conducted at least annually by compliance management or qualified third parties across all businesses and products to understand the areas of risk within your bank across the entire loan life cycle. The board of directors should review the results of the risk assessment, focusing on the gaps between the risks and controls. The risk assessment is designed to qualitatively and/or quantitatively evaluate inherent fair lending risk, the adequacy of the control environment, and any residual fair lending risk.

The risk assessment may employ a methodology that consists of a review of relevant policies, procedures, and documentation; conducting interviews with key business, compliance, legal, and lending personnel; reviewing quantitative fair lending analyses; and summarizing and validating each component of the review with appropriate personnel. A bank's risk assessment process should be tailored to the bank's size, complexity, and products and services offered. If possible, risk assessments should be performed at the direction of legal counsel to preserve the bank's attorney-client privilege of sensitive information.

2. Preventive Controls

In addition to a fair lending policy, a bank should have policies and procedures that describe how fair lending compliance is achieved at all stages of the bank's lending and servicing activities. Typically, this involves integrating fair lending concepts into key policies and procedures such as credit risk policies, pricing policies, underwriting procedures, and loss mitigation policies and procedures. Such policies should clearly allocate fair lending risk management responsibilities at all levels of the organization. Ongoing monitoring should be performed to ensure that these policies and procedures are carried out in practice. Fair lending-related policies and procedures should be reviewed at least annually by the board of directors or management, as appropriate, and enhanced for areas that are likely to be subject to regulatory scrutiny such as pricing, credit risk and underwriting, fees, customer disclosures, marketing and advertising, loss mitigation, loan modification, and foreclosure and repossession.

Preventive controls should also include annual fair lending training for all employees involved in the loan origination and servicing process, as well as management and the board of directors. Job-specific fair lending training should also be required based on the employee's job function, particularly if the role involves the exercise of judgment (*e.g.*, underwriters). Training should also be used to communicate any new fair lending-related legislative and regulatory changes.

Incentive compensation plans may also pose fair lending risk if they incentivize undesirable behavior (*e.g.*, product steering). Therefore, legal and compliance personnel should review incentive compensation for sales, underwriting, and servicing personnel at least annually to ensure that incentives are aligned with the fair lending laws. The board of directors may approve incentive compensation plans generally on an annual basis.

3. Detective Controls

Detective controls (monitoring and testing) are an important component of a bank's fair lending risk management program because they help determine whether the bank's preventive controls are working or otherwise adequate to manage fair lending risk. Detective controls include conducting ongoing monitoring and testing of automated, manual, or process-oriented controls designed to manage the use of discretion to ensure that they are effective and working as intended.

Statistical analyses and comparative file reviews (discussed in Chapter VIII) may also be conducted to compare similarly qualified applicants and borrowers and ensure that any dissimilar treatment among protected and non-protected class groups is not related to a prohibited basis in relation to the levels of assistance provided, credit decisions made, and terms and pricing granted. Any fair lending testing and monitoring should be performed on an ongoing basis in order to monitor trends and identify areas of potential regulatory scrutiny. Management-level and board risk committees should receive periodic summaries of the results as appropriate to understand areas of heightened fair lending risk.

4. Issue Identification and Corrective Action

If a potential fair lending issue is identified, it is important that the bank has a procedure for addressing and resolving the issue — and escalating it to management and the board of directors, if necessary. If a fair lending matter is escalated, management, the board of directors, or a board committee may make a decision, direct corrective action, or require further study of the matter.

A bank should maintain an issue tracking system and develop corrective action plans to ensure that each issue is resolved in a timely and appropriate manner. On a periodic basis, the status of any significant fair lending issue under management should be reported to appropriate risk committees and, if needed, the board of directors.

5. Reporting to Risk Management Committees

A bank's fair lending policy and program documentation should document an escalation and reporting process to ensure that executive management, and the board of directors, where necessary, is promptly alerted to any material issues involving fair lending non-compliance. On a periodic basis, ideally monthly or quarterly, the fair lending officer or chief compliance officer should report any significant fair lending developments to executive management and appropriate risk management committees.

6. Consumer Complaint Management

Consumer complaints are a key area of focus for the CFPB and the prudential regulators. In fact, even one complaint may lead to an investigation, targeted examination, or enforcement action. Banks should develop and maintain a robust consumer complaint management program to ensure that any fair lending complaints are properly identified, promptly responded to, and monitored or escalated, if needed. Fair lending complaints are typically reviewed and responded to by legal and/or compliance rather than the business line because of the heightened risk associated with allegations of discrimination.

To meet regulatory expectations, banks should establish a centralized system for tracking and monitoring consumer complaints (including fair lending complaints) and create periodic reports for the board of directors and any risk management committees that analyze complaint numbers, types of complaints, root causes, and trends. The board of directors should note any changes in volume and/or trends and, if needed, direct management to review policies, procedures, or practices and make any modifications necessary to address any systemic issues from an operational perspective.

7. Periodic Internal Audits

On a periodic basis (such as annually), a bank should conduct an independent audit assessing its compliance with fair lending laws and regulations. The board and audit or other board committee may be involved in setting the scope of the fair lending audit and choosing the party to conduct the audit. The audit may be conducted by either internal audit or an external auditor, but most often the internal audit group conducts fair lending audits.

The internal audit group is typically asked to audit for compliance with the fair lending policy or conduct an audit of the fair lending program to ensure that it does not create any non-attorney/client privileged materials regarding fair lending. Because of the sensitivity, confidentiality and complexity of fair lending statistical analysis, it is important that internal audit not conduct any statistical analyses of its own or evaluate fair lending regression models or results as part of the audit process.

The results from the fair lending audit should be shared with the board of directors, its audit committee, and appropriate management-level risk committees. The board and its audit committee should review the results of the audit and follow up if the results require corrective action.

CHAPTER VII.
EFFECTIVELY PREPARING FOR AND MANAGING A FAIR LENDING EXAMINATION

Banks of all sizes are subject to various types of examinations by federal and/or state regulators. Regulators use fair lending examinations to determine whether a bank is meeting its compliance responsibilities under federal or state fair lending laws and regulations. As a bank director, you are not expected to participate in the day-to-day aspects of your bank's examination process. Nonetheless, you should be familiar with the process because many fair lending enforcement actions have originated from fair lending examination findings. This Chapter discusses how a bank can effectively prepare for and manage a fair lending examination conducted by a federal regulator.

Depending on your bank's size and charter, the federal fair lending examination may be conducted by the CFPB or your bank's prudential regulator. Like other types of examinations, fair lending examinations typically consist of three primary components: (1) off-site analysis and review of information; (2) on-site examination of the bank's operations, information, and documents; and (3) the written examination report.

Regardless of which regulator conducts your bank's fair lending examination, the key to a successful outcome to any bank examination is careful planning, preparation, and effective regulatory relationship management.[61] Below we provide some practical guidance on what to expect in a fair lending examination by your prudential regulator or the

CFPB, and what your bank can do before, during, and after an on-site fair lending examination to ensure that the examination is managed properly and yields the best results possible.[62]

A. How to Effectively Prepare for a Fair Lending Examination

In order to become familiar with the examination process, your bank's fair lending compliance staff should start by reviewing the relevant examination procedures from the CFPB or applicable prudential regulator, depending upon which regulator is responsible for conducting your bank's fair lending examination. Although all of the federal regulators base their exam procedures on the Interagency Fair Lending Examination Procedures created by the Federal Financial Institution Examination Council, each regulator takes a slightly different approach. Therefore, it is important for your compliance staff to be familiar with the entire set of examination procedures for your primary fair lending regulator.

Your bank's legal department should also stay abreast of new and revised fair lending laws, regulations, and other relevant regulatory guidance. It is important to be aware of areas where the regulators have expressed concern because these are likely to be areas of focus during the examination. For example, in the CFPB's recent Fair Lending Report to Congress, the agency reaffirmed mortgage lending and auto finance as its top priorities for its supervisory and enforcement work for the second consecutive year. With respect to mortgage lending, the CFPB estimates that it has conducted targeted ECOA reviews of institutions responsible for approximately 40% of HMDA-reportable applications and originations.[63] The CFPB also noted its ongoing supervision and enforcement in other markets, and specifically unsecured lending.[64]

Knowing your regulator's priorities can help your bank proactively assess whether its controls and programs are consistent with regulatory expectations and industry best practices. Knowing these priorities can also help your bank anticipate any potential concerns that could be raised by the examiners.

Regulators use a risk-based prioritization process to determine which legal entities and/or products pose the greatest risk of lending discrimination. Factors that feed into this process may include fair lending complaints, public or private litigation, information gathered from prior fair lending examinations or enforcement actions, the adequacy and quality of your bank's fair lending program, quantitative analyses, and research or insight from the CFPB's Research, Markets, and Regulations division. Before the examination gets underway, your bank should ensure that it has appropriately addressed any issues with its programs, policies, or controls that may have been cited in past examinations, audits, or risk assessments.

Even if your bank has not received notice of a fair lending examination, it is not too early to begin pulling and organizing documents, such as policies and procedures, which are likely to be requested by the examiners. This is because the regulators may not give your bank ample notice of a fair lending examination. In the same vein, to the extent your bank becomes aware of weaknesses that a regulator is likely to discover, legal and compliance staff should consider preparing draft narrative responses in advance.

Areas within your bank that present high fair lending risk should receive special attention. As a bank director, you should be apprised of those issues, and potentially participate in intensive briefings with senior management. We have seen examination outcomes that have been undermined when bank directors could not answer basic questions by examiners or discuss issues with examiners that board minutes indicated were the subject of deliberation and action.

Furthermore, it is not too early for compliance staff to provide examination management training for employees who may interface with examiners and to identify the person who will serve as the day-to-day contact for the examiners. In addition, examiners are increasingly meeting with individual members of the board or the board as a whole to discuss examination issues. Therefore, those board members need to prepare thoroughly for such meetings.

As a bank director, it is important to know that certain information that examiners request may be protected by the attorney-client privilege. Banks should identify documents as privileged, where appropriate, when producing them to the regulators to avoid waiving the privilege with respect to third parties. Although generally most information and document requests in the examination context are not subject to typical privilege protections, to the extent that they are, the production of information or documents to the CFPB, or any regulator for that matter, does not waive any privilege that may be claimed with respect to third parties.[65]

B. How to Effectively Manage the Fair Lending Examination Process

Even though the board of directors typically does not get involved in day-to-day management of a fair lending examination, bank directors should receive periodic updates about the examination from compliance and legal staff.

During the examination, your bank's regulatory relationship manager should be the central point of contact for the examiner in charge. In smaller institutions, that person may be a very senior officer, including the CEO. Banks should engage in a dialogue with the examiners early and often throughout the examination, especially so you can promptly respond to any potential issues or weaknesses cited by the examiners. Early notice from an examiner that a violation may have occurred will allow your bank to provide the examiner with additional information that may address the concern or demonstrate that there was no violation, clarify any misunderstanding that the examiner may have, or alert you to a previously unidentified issue that the bank can begin to investigate.

Even though the bank may have a good relationship with the examiner, it is important to treat all responses to the examiner's questions, no matter how informal the communication, as a formal inquiry. It is important to ensure that all requests are appropriately reviewed and considered, and that all responses are complete, accurate, and subject to review by the appropriate bank personnel, especially legal and compliance staff. When having discussions of crucial importance relating to the examination in which a written response is not required, it is still beneficial to document the conversation in writing by either sending a letter or email to the examiner, drafting an internal memorandum to file, or taking contemporaneous notes of the conversation.

C. "Soft" Exit Meeting

At the end of the examination, it is customary for the regulators to hold a "soft" exit meeting, where the examiners will preview their preliminary findings (which may include potential violations of law) that they intend to memorialize in the final report. Banks should use the soft exit meeting as an opportunity to discuss in depth the issues examiners have identified during the examination. It is important for your bank to recognize that these findings are not necessarily final. The final outcome could be changed, especially if the examiners' findings are based on a misunderstanding of the facts. Your bank would want to learn, if possible, any intent by the examiners to refer a matter to DOJ or recommend an enforcement action. If your bank learns of this intent, it will allow the bank to prepare a detailed written response to the examiners' concerns before the referral or recommendation is actually made.

To the extent that your bank does not agree with the examiners' preliminary findings or statement of the facts, your bank should advocate for a more accurate or favorable result by clarifying any misunderstanding in writing that the examiners may have or providing in writing any additional information to justify another result.

D. What to Do After the Regulators Have Left

Through the process of engaging the examiner during the on-site examination and information learned during the soft exit meeting, your bank should be able to anticipate what some of the findings will be. Furthermore, to the extent you know or expect the final examination report will likely require certain changes, keep in mind that the final examination report may not give your bank very much time to implement the changes. As such, your bank will only benefit by taking advantage of the additional time and commencing corrective action and/or consumer remediation promptly.

A bank may be able to change the final result of the examination if it can quickly and effectively address any deficiencies identified during the soft exit meeting. Sometimes examiners may modify the language their reports if they observe that the bank has made meaningful progress toward resolving the finding.

E. "Official" Exit Meeting

At the official exit meeting, the regulators will typically issue their final observations in an examination report. Depending on the nature of the examiners' findings or scope of the examination, a supervisory letter may be issued instead of a full report of examination. Unlike the soft exit meeting, there is no opportunity for a bank to advocate for changes in the document because the results have been memorialized in a final report or letter.

If the board of directors and/or management team disagree with the findings of the examination report, an appeals process may be available depending on the finding that your bank wishes to dispute. It is advisable to consult your internal or external legal counsel concerning how the process works and whether your institution can avail itself of the appeals process under the circumstances presented. Banks may also avail themselves of the agency's office of the ombudsman to seek informal guidance, ask for information about the appeals process, or have the ombudsman serve as a neutral facilitator for communication between the bank and the agency. The appeals process will vary depending on your bank's prudential regulator. The OCC's Ombudsman, for instance, has authority to make binding decisions. The role of Ombudsman is somewhat different for the FRB and the FDIC. Those agencies have committees that will consider an appeal, and their Ombudsmen serve as liaisons to the agency and the bank throughout that process.

Following the issuance of the examination report, the board's role is to provide guidance to management and assistance in determining whether to pursue an appeal.

CHAPTER VIII.
HMDA – GETTING IT RIGHT AND KNOWING YOUR DATA

HMDA was enacted by Congress in 1975 in response to the rising public concern that financial institutions were not meeting the mortgage loan needs of certain urban neighborhoods. HMDA and its implementing regulation, Regulation C, are designed to provide a reporting mechanism that allows financial institutions, regulators, and the public at large to determine whether financial institutions are failing to meet the housing needs of their communities and/or are engaging in discriminatory lending practices.

In 2011, the Dodd-Frank Act transferred rulemaking authority under HMDA from the FRB to the CFPB. The CFPB now shares enforcement authority for HMDA with the FRB, OCC, FDIC, NCUA, and HUD. As discussed in this Chapter, the agencies have placed great emphasis on accurate HMDA data and entered into public and non-public enforcement actions against banks and non-banks that have failed to provide those data.

As further discussed in this Chapter, the CFPB and prudential regulators use HMDA data as a screening mechanism for fair lending examinations to determine areas of mortgage lending risk.

A. HMDA Compliance Requirements

1. Data Collection, Reporting, and Public Disclosure

HMDA disclosure requirements apply to banks, savings associations and credit unions, and state-licensed mortgage lenders. A lender may be exempt from HMDA reporting based on its asset size, location, or volume of residential mortgage lending.

Every year, lenders that are subject to HMDA must record and disclose certain information regarding applications for, and originations and purchases of, home purchase loans, home improvement loans, and refinances. Lenders must also report information on applications that did not result in originations; these include denials, incomplete applications, and applications that the lender approved but the applicant chose not to accept.

Data must be collected on a loan-by-loan or application-by-application basis and compiled into a loan application register ("LAR").[66] The Federal Financial Institutions Examination Council ("FFIEC"), in turn, uses the LAR data and produces aggregate level tables incorporating geographic information by metropolitan statistical areas ("MSAs") and census tracts defined by the United States Census Bureau. The LAR data are often referred to as "HMDA data." HMDA data are intended to show lending patterns by property location, age of housing stock, income level, sex, ethnicity, and race.

2. Data Accuracy

As the agency with rulemaking authority for HMDA, the CFPB has emphasized in its guidance that accurate HMDA data is vital to carrying out the purposes of the statute. Lenders required to file a LAR pursuant to HMDA and Regulation C[67] should therefore take active steps to implement an appropriate and effective compliance management system to ensure data accuracy. According to the CFPB, an effective HMDA compliance management system generally has the following attributes:

- Comprehensive policies, procedures, and internal controls to ensure ongoing HMDA and Regulation C compliance.

- Pre-submission HMDA audits that evaluate data accuracy and recommend corrective action as needed.

- Ongoing monitoring to keep the institution apprised of any regulatory changes that may have occurred since the last data collection cycle and/or supervisory examination.

- Employees who are specifically responsible for HMDA compliance, and who receive periodic and appropriate training regarding HMDA and Regulation C standards.

- Appropriate oversight by the institution's board of directors and senior management.[68]

It is the responsibility of the board of directors and senior management to oversee that their institution develops and maintains a HMDA compliance management system that is appropriately tailored to the size, scope, and complexity of the entity's lending operations.

Recognizing that most LARs will contain some errors, the CFPB has established thresholds for error rates to determine when an institution must resubmit its LAR. In the event that a lender reports inaccurate HMDA data, resubmission of the data is only required if the number of errors exceeds a certain threshold amount.[69]

3. Enforcement of HMDA and Regulation C

Compliance with HMDA is enforced by the CFPB, FRB, OCC, FDIC, NCUA, and HUD. Failure to record or submit accurate HMDA data can result in administrative enforcement action being taken against the financial institution, including civil money penalties.

In deciding whether or not to pursue a public enforcement action for a violation of HMDA, the CFPB considers all relevant factors, including the size of an institution's LAR and the observed error rate; whether an institution self-identified its LAR errors outside of the examination context and independently took corrective action; and, for institutions that have previously been on notice of LAR errors, whether error rates have increased or have decreased sufficiently to show substantial progress in improving HMDA compliance management.

The CFPB has already shown its willingness to use civil money penalties as an enforcement tool for HMDA violations. In 2013, the CFPB required two mortgage lenders to pay civil money penalties of $34,000 and $425,000, respectively, in response to their submission of inaccurate HMDA data.[70] The CFPB also ordered both lenders to correct and resubmit their HMDA data and develop and implement an effective compliance management system to prevent future violations. Notably, the consent order against Washington Federal contains a section that pertains specifically to the role of the board of directors in overseeing compliance with the required actions.[71]

Given the potential costs arising from a HMDA violation and the requirement to resubmit a filing, financial institutions subject to HMDA's reporting requirements should make it a priority to develop and maintain an effective HMDA compliance management system, as described above. Although Regulation C contains a provision on bona fide errors, which provides that an error in compiling or recording HMDA data is not considered a violation if it was unintentional and occurred despite the existence and maintenance of procedures reasonably designed to prevent such errors,[72] an error rate that exceeds the permissible thresholds would most likely result in a determination that the institution's procedures were not reasonably designed to prevent such errors. It is the board of directors' role to ensure that your bank maintains a robust compliance management system with sufficient staffing and resources, as well as employee HMDA compliance training, to significantly reduce HMDA data errors, which in turn lessens the chance of a HMDA violation.

B. Supervisory Use of HMDA Data

1. Fair Lending Examinations

Regulators regularly use HMDA data in connection with mortgage-related fair lending and CRA examinations, so it is important for your bank to routinely run its own analysis of its HMDA data (at least annually or perhaps quarterly) to understand and defend it. Because HMDA data are not comprehensive — for example, it currently does not show the creditworthiness of the borrower associated with a given reportable loan — regulators typically use the data as a screening mechanism to look for potential fair lending issues, rather than as the ultimate basis for an examination finding of discrimination or an enforcement action. By running your own HMDA analyses, the bank can point to other factors involved in a particular credit decision or pricing that the HMDA data may not reflect, such as FICO score or loan-to-value ratio, for example.

Examiners, for instance, often rely upon HMDA data to determine which areas of an institution's lending operations appear to result in disparate treatment of prohibited basis group borrowers or applicants. An examiner might run statistical analyses of an entity's HMDA data to evaluate, for example, the denial rate for minority applicants as compared with control denial rates. If there is a statistically significant difference between the two denial rates, the examiner would then review and compare loan files before making an examination finding of discrimination.

Examiners also rely upon HMDA data to support inferences that banks may be engaging in redlining in certain metropolitan regions. In these cases, the regulator will utilize a bank's HMDA data to determine the bank's application volume in majority-minority census tracts compared to non-majority-minority census tracts. If it appears that a bank is serving predominantly minority neighborhoods significantly less than predominantly white neighborhoods, the regulators may perceive this as evidence of potential redlining.

There are several potential defenses that a lender could assert in response to a regulatory or enforcement agency's claims of redlining or other discriminatory lending practices on the basis of HMDA data. First, a lender can point out the incomplete nature of HMDA data, which fail to include information regarding borrower creditworthiness, housing prices, collateral values, or credit scores. HMDA data also fails to reflect the full range of a bank's lending activities. To address the deficiencies in publicly available data, regulatory agencies routinely ask for "HMDA plus" data prior to an examination, which would include the types of data listed above. If an inquiry arises from circumstances other than an examination, preliminary analyses may be based only on data in the public LAR, which limits the reliability of any statistical results. Whether a fair lending claim is raised by a regulator or enforcement agency, institutions should develop their own competing analyses (and conduct file reviews, where appropriate) to try and demonstrate the non-discriminatory reasons for the perceived disparate treatment or disparate impact.

2. Transactions Requiring Supervisory Approval

Regulators also consider HMDA data when approving or disapproving applications submitted by banks seeking to engage in certain transactions, including establishing new branches or merging with another institution, as described below.

Branching

When determining whether or not to approve a bank's application to establish additional branch offices, regulators often consider the bank's compliance with the fair lending laws. This may include an analysis of HMDA data, particularly if public comments have been submitted in response to the application that include arguments based upon HMDA data. However, the regulators acknowledge that critical data regarding a bank's lending decisions are not reported under HMDA, and may seek to supplement their analysis accordingly with a bank's internal analysis reflecting HMDA plus data or additional, non-HMDA-based reasoning.

In order to facilitate a regulatory decision regarding a branching application, a bank should be prepared to provide the regulators with additional statistical analyses and reports based upon HMDA plus data and other proprietary information pertaining to its lending operations. This additional information may refute or explain any problematic HMDA statistics relied upon by the agency.

Mergers

Regulators also consider HMDA data when making a determination regarding an application to combine two institutions. As with applications for additional branches, regulators may directly address HMDA data in their analysis, especially in response to public comments based upon HMDA statistics. Applicant banks seeking approval to merge should be able to provide the regulators with their own statistical analyses and reports based upon non-HMDA data to demonstrate compliance with fair lending and CRA requirements. When one bank in a proposed merger has been cited with a fair lending violation, the regulator typically focuses on whether the other bank in the proposed merger has a robust fair lending compliance program that is equipped to address any potential deficiencies at the other institution. When both banks involved in a proposed merger are addressing fair lending violations or investigations, this factor generally serves as an impediment to approval of the merger until one or both issues are resolved.

C. Public Use of HMDA Data

1. Private Litigation

Private litigants — individuals and groups — also rely on publicly available HMDA data in pursuing discrimination claims against lenders. In the past, class action suits have been filed against mortgage lenders based upon HMDA statistical analyses that appeared to suggest that minority mortgage applicants were treated less favorably than white applicants.

For example, in *Ramirez v. GreenPoint Mortgage Funding, Inc.,*[73] three minority borrowers who obtained mortgage loans from GreenPoint Mortgage Funding ("GreenPoint") brought a class action alleging that GreenPoint violated the FHA and ECOA by charging minority borrowers disproportionately high rates compared to non-minority borrowers with the same credit risk profile. The plaintiffs successfully made a prima facie case that alleged pricing discrimination occurred on the basis of statistical analyses of HMDA data,[74] and GreenPoint subsequently settled for $14.75 million.

The fact that public HMDA data alone cannot be used to comprehensively analyze a bank's lending practices, however, proves to be a significant challenge for private litigants whose primary source of empirical evidence is HMDA data.

Banks frequently defend against HMDA-based claims by questioning the validity of any conclusions drawn without critical information regarding borrower and collateral. However, challenging the validity of a complainant's statistical results is generally effective only if the lender can propose a more robust data set or model that disproves a statistically significant disparity.

2. Community Group Action

Since the 1990s, community groups have used HMDA data to investigate, publicize, and combat perceived discriminatory lending patterns, particularly in urban areas with a significant minority population. Community groups have relied upon a variety of approaches to accomplish their goals, including protests to applications for mergers or acquisitions, administrative complaints, public awareness campaigns, complaints to financial regulators and enforcement agencies, and private agreements with financial institutions. While community groups frequently rely on the statistical analysis of publicly available HMDA data to support their fair lending claims, they sometimes support such claims by conducting "mystery shopping."

Example: St. Louis Metropolitan Area

The St. Louis, Missouri metropolitan area has long been the focus of community group pressure based on HMDA data. Since the Association of Community Organizers for Reform Now ("ACORN") launched its first anti-redlining campaign in St. Louis in 1976, lenders in the St. Louis area have found themselves the subjects of ongoing fair lending scrutiny based upon their HMDA data. Even after decades of negotiations and agreements between local community groups and St. Louis-area mortgage lenders, claims of redlining and other fair lending concerns persist.

A settlement between the Metropolitan St. Louis Equal Housing Opportunity Council ("Metropolitan St. Louis EHOC") and First National Bank of St. Louis ("FNBSL") indicates that community groups in St. Louis remain active in their pursuit of fair lending reform at local financial institutions. This agreement, which was approved by HUD in 2010, resolved a complaint filed by Metropolitan St. Louis EHOC alleging that FNBSL excluded areas with a high concentration of minorities in its lending operations and branch office offerings.[75] As part of the settlement, FNBSL was required to implement a variety of outreach, educational, and special financing initiatives directed toward minority communities in the St. Louis metropolitan region.

The St. Louis metropolitan area example serves as a reminder to the leadership of financial institutions, particularly those in urban areas, that community groups remain powerful advocacy forces in the area of fair lending. The board and senior management of financial institutions located in geographic areas with a strong community group presence should be open to dialogue with these groups outside of the regulatory context.

Privately-negotiated partnerships with community groups can serve to improve access to credit for minorities, enhance an institution's local reputation, reduce fair lending risk, and avoid administrative intervention and/or costly litigation expenses.

D. The Future of HMDA Data

As technology reduces the burdens of accessing and analyzing HMDA data for individuals and community groups, lenders should expect that fair lending challenges based upon HMDA information will continue in the future.

The Dodd-Frank Act amends HMDA to require banks to collect and report additional information for purchased and originated loans. These enhanced collection and reporting requirements become effective after the CFPB publishes a final rule to implement these changes. In October 2015, the CFPB issued a final rule that substantially expands the scope of HMDA data reporting requirements.[76]

While some of the CFPB's new requirements were expressly mandated by the Dodd-Frank Act, the CFPB also adopted a significant number of new data points based on its discretionary rulemaking authority granted by the Dodd-Frank Act. See Appendix C for a list of the current and amended data collection requirements. The availability of such "HMDA-plus data" is likely to ignite increased enforcement and litigation activity.

In 2013, the CFPB unveiled a web-based tool aimed at providing consumers with online, user-friendly access to HMDA data.[77] Individuals browsing the CFPB's website can sort publicly-available HMDA data into maps and charts, which could be used to identify potential discriminatory trends or practices. One potential outgrowth of the new HMDA data tool may be increased consumer and community group interaction with HMDA data, which may give rise to discrimination complaints and/or fair lending-related litigation.

CHAPTER IX.
AN INTRODUCTION TO FAIR LENDING STATISTICAL ANALYSES – MAKING SENSE OF YOUR BANK'S DATA

In recent years, fair lending monitoring and testing has become a regulatory expectation for banks of all sizes. Likewise, regulators, private plaintiffs, and consumer advocacy groups are using statistical evidence to support their discrimination claims for both mortgage and non-mortgage products. Regulators also rely on statistical analyses prior to examinations in order to determine a focal point for the examination and during the examination to identify potential fair lending violations. The CFPB in particular has publicly stated that it is using a "data-driven" approach to shape its supervisory and enforcement priorities at both the bank and market levels.[78]

As a bank director, you are not responsible for managing the day-to-day aspects of your bank's fair lending analytical program. However, you are expected to understand your bank's fair lending risk profile and what controls are in place to identify and address those risks. To effectively execute those responsibilities, it is useful for you to have a basic understanding of how statistical methods are being used to assess and enforce compliance with fair lending laws and regulations. The purpose of this Chapter is to provide you with that understanding.

A. Why Your Bank Should Consider Conducting Fair Lending Statistical Analyses

Today, many banks incorporate monitoring and testing into their fair lending compliance programs to better understand their fair lending risks and how the data could be used by regulators, private plaintiffs, and consumer advocates to allege potential violations of the fair lending laws. As discussed in Chapters III and IV, fair lending risk may be associated with your bank's products, lending channels, lending and servicing practices, and marketing efforts.

Using statistical analyses, your bank can develop a risk-based approach to ensure that priority is given to areas within the bank that present the highest quantitative fair lending risk. In Chapter VI, we discussed the importance of establishing policies, procedures, and other controls to mitigate fair lending risk across your bank's credit business. Statistical analyses can be used, in part, to test the effectiveness of those controls.

In the litigation and enforcement context, most fair lending allegations involve claims that a bank did not apply its lending policies and practices equally to similarly situated applicants or borrowers. However, banks that take a deeper dive into their data may successfully rebut these allegations by finding flaws in the claimant's statistical analysis and presenting an alternative analysis that shows that the policy or practice at issue was not discriminatory.

It is important to recognize that there is no "one size fits all" formula for developing a bank's fair lending statistical analysis program. Ultimately, the analyses that your bank performs (and the frequency in which they are performed) will depend on myriad factors, including your bank's size, complexity, product mix, loan volume, risk appetite, and resources.

B. Collection and Use of Data for Fair Lending Statistical Analyses

Fair lending professionals frequently quote the old adage "garbage in, garbage out," which means that imperfect data will lead to imperfect results. There are several reasons why compilation of data for fair lending analysis is challenging.

First, data is not always available or easily accessible. For instance, it may be difficult or impossible to account for critical factors in a statistical analysis because those factors are qualitative in nature (*e.g.,* conversations with underwriters which are memorialized in loan files) or because the data simply may not exist (*e.g.,* race, ethnicity, and sex cannot be collected by law for non-mortgage credit products).

Second, data integrity may also present obstacles to an accurate statistical result, particularly where multiple systems have conflicting data. For instance, the reliability and completeness of the available data may be compromised due to human data entry errors. So while statistical analyses can provide helpful insight into a bank's fair lending risk, those results are only as good as the underlying data.

In general, there are two sources of prohibited basis group data that are used to conduct fair lending statistical analyses: (1) HMDA data for mortgage loans, and (2) proxy data for non-mortgage loans.

1. Using HMDA Data

In accordance with Regulation B, mortgage lenders must ask (but not require) applicants to identify their ethnicity, race, sex, and marital status when applying for a loan secured by a dwelling that is occupied (or will be occupied) by the applicant.[79] Borrower demographic data that is compiled and reported pursuant to HMDA and Regulation C include only race, ethnicity, and sex for the applicant and co-applicant.[80] HMDA data are used by regulators, consumer advocacy groups, and private plaintiffs to "assist in identifying possible discriminatory lending patterns and enforcing antidiscrimination statutes."[81]

Using HMDA data, a regulator could develop a statistical model to identify potential differences in mortgage loan pricing for minority borrowers and non-Hispanic white borrowers. Today's HMDA data do not incorporate many non-discriminatory and objective factors used by a bank to evaluate any given loan application, such as the applicant's credit score, the applicant's debt-to-income ratio, or the loan-to-value ratio. Even though the CFPB's new HMDA collection and reporting requirements[82] are expected to address some of these limitations, other issues involving data availability and data integrity will remain.

83

2. Using Other Data Sources

Data collection for non-mortgage credit products can be particularly challenging because fair lending laws and regulations prohibit lenders from collecting data on race, ethnicity, sex, and other prohibited basis characteristics for these applicants.[83] In the absence of data linked to applicants' or borrowers' protected class status, proxies must be used to estimate the ethnicity, race, sex, and other protected group characteristics for non-mortgage loan applicants.

For example, regulators use a proxy methodology that predicts the likelihood of an applicant being Hispanic or Asian based on his or her surname. Because surname proxies are particularly poor predictors of race, regulators typically use census tract data to predict the likelihood of an applicant being African American. An applicant's sex is typically predicted by use of first name proxies.

In three recent indirect auto enforcement actions,[84] the CFPB and DOJ used a proxy methodology that stems from the health care industry called Bayesian Improved Surname Geocoding ("BISG") that estimates race and ethnicity of a borrower based on a combination of geocoding and surname data.[85] In September 2014, the CFPB recently issued a "white paper" to provide more detail on its BISG proxy methodology.[86]

Even though the use of proxies can be a helpful monitoring tool, there is ample evidence that proxy methodologies frequently fail to accurately predict an applicant's or borrower's characteristics. To the contrary, an article on the predictive strength of the BISG methodology concluded that there was only a 76% correlation between the assigned BISG proxy and the self-reported race or ethnicity of the subjects.[87]

Similarly, a 2014 study conducted by Charles River Associates that was commissioned by the American Financial Services Association ("AFSA") regarding indirect auto retail installment sales contracts found that the BISG proxy methodology resulted in significant bias and high error rates.[88] AFSA's study calculated BISG probabilities against a test population of HMDA data, where actual race and ethnicity are known. Those results revealed that BISG fails to identify three out of four African American applicants and four out of 10 Hispanic applicants.[89] The AFSA study concluded that while the BISG proxy methodology "may be relatively less inaccurate than geography-only and name-only proxy methods, the methodology is characterized by objectively high error rates."[90]

C. Using Statistical Analyses to Assess Your Bank's Fair Lending Performance

1. Understanding the Types of Fair Lending Reviews

There are two common tools used in fair lending statistical reviews that can help a lender identify potential fair lending risk: regression analysis and file reviews. These reviews can help a lender identify differences in credit decision or pricing outcomes and the factors that may be driving those differences. Regression analysis is a statistical analysis of loan data for a particular lending channel (*e.g.*, mortgage, credit card, auto) that is further segmented by loan product (*e.g.*, prime vs. nonprime or conforming vs. non-conforming).

Unlike a "raw" statistical analysis that only looks for disparities without any explanatory variables, a regression model will take into account important explanatory variables that may have impacted the pricing or underwriting decision, including credit score, property type, debt-to-income ratio, loan-to-value ratio, and prior bankruptcies or foreclosures. By analyzing the data with a regression model, lenders are evaluating applicants in an "apples-to-apples" approach.

Where the results of a regression analysis show that there is a statistically significant disparity in pricing or underwriting that is adverse to a prohibited basis group, lenders commonly elect to review loan files for three reasons.

First, the files may reveal that certain data fields were excluded from the regression model that have a material impact on the statistical results. Second, the files may show legitimate non-discriminatory reasons for the decisions that are not captured in the loan data (*e.g.*, ineligible collateral, failure to provide the necessary documentation to complete the application process, appraisal value did not support the requested loan amount, etc.). Third, the file review may identify that there is a data integrity issue (*e.g.*, the decline reason in the data does not reflect the decline reason in the loan file).

Regression Analysis

A regression analysis is a commonly used technique in fair lending statistical analysis. It is a technique used for studying the relationships between the various underwriting, pricing, and personal criteria that form the basis of a bank's underwriting or pricing decision. In other words, regression analyses can help explain why credit and pricing decisions are made.

Even where the results of a regression analysis show indicia of discrimination, it does not mean that discrimination actually occurred. As a result, file reviews are typically conducted as a follow-up to the results of an initial regression analysis.

Historically, fair lending regression analyses alone have not been considered sufficient evidence to establish a discrimination claim by a regulator or enforcement agency. However, the CFPB has recently been pursuing fair lending investigations against lenders where the results of a regression analysis alone have formed the basis of an allegation.

As explained below, file reviews are an essential element of a fair lending analysis insofar as critical information can derive from this type of review that cannot be obtained solely through a statistical analysis.

File Reviews

Where outliers are identified in a regression analysis, a file review can be a helpful tool in determining whether the loan files reveal legitimate and non-discriminatory reasons to explain the differential treatment of applicants or borrowers that cannot be captured in the data. As noted above, a file review may reveal potential data integrity issues or data points that were omitted from the regression model that may be an appropriate variable to include.

File reviews typically involve a review of any hard copy or electronic loan files, including notes and emails, as well as the data and information stored in the loan origination system. The objective of such reviews is to determine whether there are non-discriminatory reasons to explain the differences observed in the statistical analysis. It is possible that some of these differences could not have been factored into a quantitative model.

File reviewers may also need to conduct interviews of loan originators or underwriters for added context, particularly where the documentation in the file is sparse. In some cases, a bank may need to consult with a third party engaged in the origination process, such as a mortgage broker or auto lender, for information about the credit decision or pricing outcome. Ideally, supplemental interviews would not be necessary because the loan files should be well-documented and provide enough detail to explain credit decisions or pricing outcomes, but such documentation is often limited.

It is important to train file reviewers about the requisite information to collect during the file review and how that information should be captured in the results. If analysis is required by the file reviewer, the file reviewer should not be asked to determine whether there is evidence of discrimination, which is only appropriate for legal counsel. The file reviewer should only be determining whether there is evidence in the file to support the pricing or underwriting decision.

Comparative File Reviews

In some instances, a bank may elect only to review "outlier files," which, in the context of underwriting, are the prohibited basis group applications that the regression model predicted to be approved but were declined, and the control group applications that the model predicted to be declined but were approved. For pricing, outlier files may be reviewed for prohibited basis group applicants where the regression model predicted pricing that is less than the actual price given to the protected basis group applicant and the predicted pricing for control group applicants is more than the pricing actually provided to the control group applicant.

Regulators tend to prefer comparative file reviews, which look at a sample of outlier files from a prohibited basis group and similarly situated control group borrowers to serve as comparators. The objective is to determine whether similarly situated applicants received similar treatment during the pricing or underwriting process.

As an initial step, the bank must choose the appropriate focal points for the review. The most meaningful comparative file reviews hone in on a specific loan product, time frame, geographic region, or phase of the credit administration process.

Next, the bank should identify the appropriate sample of loans, which is usually accomplished by focusing on marginal applicants or borrowers. Marginal applicants consist of approved and denied applications that were not clearly qualified or unqualified based on the bank's underwriting criteria.

These include, among other things, applications that a more conservative loan officer might have denied, applications that narrowly met or failed the bank's written guidelines, and applications for which certain creditworthiness requirements may have been waived. FFIEC has published guidance on suggested sample sizes for comparative file reviews, which the CFPB has subsequently incorporated into its examination procedures.[91]

The file review itself compares files of individuals who belong to a protected class group (*e.g.*, women, racial or ethnic minorities) to files of individuals who are not members of a protected class. When identifying the focal points for the review, the bank should limit each review to the comparison of one protected class group. To illustrate, one review should compare the treatment of males to females, rather than compare the treatment of non-Hispanic white males to Hispanic females.

When conducting the review, a best practice is to document the reviewer's findings in a spreadsheet. With respect to each applicant or borrower, the spreadsheet should set forth the data points that are used in the credit decision or pricing process (*e.g.*, FICO, trade history, date of action, loan amount, loan-to-value ratio ("LTV"), debt-to-income ratio, etc.) as well as notes in contained in the file that could justify the final outcome (*e.g.*, policy exceptions or compensating factors).

2. Using Statistical Analyses Across Your Bank's Credit Administration Process

Underwriting Analyses

Statistical analyses of your bank's underwriting data can help answer the question of whether applicants were subject to less favorable underwriting standards or practices because of their race, color, national origin, marital status, or some other prohibited basis. There are several types of underwriting analyses that a bank could perform.

"Accept or deny" analyses could be performed to determine whether a bank denied applications from potentially qualified protected class members but approved those from similarly situated non-protected class members. A regression model would take into account the effect of objective factors that would likely influence the underwriting outcome.

Objective factors include the characteristics of the loan (*e.g.*, LTV ratio, loan type, and requested term), characteristics of the property (*e.g.*, single-family primary residence, vacation condominium, or cooperative apartment), and characteristics of the applicant (*e.g.*, creditworthiness and income).

For areas of a bank's underwriting process that afford employee discretion, such as underwriting exceptions, statistical analyses could be performed to see whether applicants of a particular demographic are more likely to receive concessions than other applicants.

"Assistance" analyses could also be performed to assess whether similarly situated applicants received different treatment in the underwriting process. A fair lending assistance case could allege that a lender made special efforts to qualify and approve non-Hispanic white mortgage applicants but did not make the same efforts for African American and Hispanic applicants.

Pricing Analyses

Statistical analyses of your bank's pricing data can help answer the question of whether borrowers received less favorable pricing terms (*e.g.*, interest rate, broker fees, overages, or other charges) because of their race, color, national origin, marital status, or some other prohibited basis.

There are a number of legitimate and non-discriminatory factors that could influence the ultimate pricing of a loan:

credit score, loan term, loan amount, LTV ratio, and geographic variables (*e.g.*, loans sorted by state or metropolitan statistical area ("MSA") or branch location). These factors should be considered in the regression model, to the extent there is data.

It is a best practice to include a timing component in the regression model (*i.e.*, interest rate lock date or loan origination date) to account for fluctuations in interest rates and market conditions. For analyses of auto loans, a regression analysis should also distinguish between new and used vehicles, and include the model year of the collateral.

Redlining Analyses

Redlining cases assert that a lender has served mostly minority geographic areas (referred to as "majority-minority") less favorably than majority-white areas. A majority-minority area is an area in which more than 50 percent of the residents identify their race or ethnicity as other than non-Hispanic white. A bank can perform redlining analyses by focusing on a single city or the larger MSA that includes a city's surrounding suburbs, then examine the populations at the census tract level. A lender's self-delineated assessment area for purposes of the CRA can also serve as the appropriate area for a redlining review.

Reverse Redlining Analyses

Reverse redlining claims arise when banks steer minority borrowers to different programs within a loan type (*e.g.*, prime versus non-prime auto loans) with less favorable terms, conditions, or pricing to otherwise qualified borrowers on a prohibited basis.

A bank may conduct analyses to assess whether it made a higher proportion of nonprime loans in majority-minority areas because of nondiscriminatory, legitimate considerations. Reverse redlining analyses may consider lending activity at both the community and borrower levels. As a result, some of the analyses in reverse redlining reviews will resemble the analyses conducted in underwriting and pricing cases.

Servicing Analyses

Because fair servicing is a relatively new concept, regulatory expectations and best practices in monitoring fair servicing compliance continue to evolve. It is worth noting that there are a number of impediments to the statistical analysis of loan servicing (*e.g.*, data limitations, borrower incentives, and action or inaction, and investor and contractual limitations) that complicate analyses of fair servicing performance.

A bank may conduct testing and monitoring to identify statistically significant unexplained disparate loan servicing and loss mitigation outcomes between borrower groups. A bank can select similarly situated borrowers and compare levels of assistance, default servicing outcome, and modification terms. Analysis of outcomes should include the range of workout possibilities and examine the frequency, the terms, and the speed of outcomes.

A bank should also examine data related to borrowers' loss mitigation behaviors (*e.g.*, whether a borrower completes a loss mitigation package, responds to follow-up inquiries by the servicer, or accepts and abides by the terms of a proposed loss mitigation program).

3. What Should Be Done With the Results of Your Bank's Statistical Analyses?

There are several options that your bank should consider if the results of the statistical analyses — after completion of any supplemental file reviews and investigation — suggest that disparate impact or disparate treatment may exist. For example, your bank may determine that corrective action or changes to the bank's policies and practices are warranted.

Legal or compliance personnel may issue warnings to loan officers, branches, or brokers with disparities in their lending practices and place these parties on a "watch list" until these disparities have been removed. Further, it may be determined that enhancements should be made to the bank's policies or procedures to ensure the consistent and objective treatment of applicants and borrowers in lending and servicing decisions.

With respect to specific borrowers, upon further review, the bank may decide that corrective action or remediation is necessary. The CFPB has encouraged banks to fully remediate customers affected by compliance issues in addition to taking action to correct the underlying deficiencies that gave rise to the remediation.[92] To that end, we are aware of banks that have proactively compensated borrowers based on the results of statistical analyses evidencing disparate pricing of loans. We recommend working with legal counsel to discuss potential options for carrying out the remediation of borrowers.

D. Who Should Perform Your Bank's Statistical Analyses?

There are several factors that your bank should consider when deciding whether to conduct statistical analyses in-house or to outsource the process. If your bank conducts statistical analyses in-house, you should consider the expertise of your personnel, cost of purchasing software, and the bank's total number of applicant and borrower files. Even though there are many software packages that can help a bank perform statistical analyses, your bank should have an in-house expert in statistics, who can assist representatives in legal and compliance in interpreting the results from the analyses.

If you engage a third-party consultant to conduct your bank's statistical analyses, you should consider whether you will be able to explain the results of these analyses to your regulator and whether you could reuse the model developed. While there are certainly advantages and disadvantages to each approach, some banks use a hybrid model in which fair lending statistical analyses are initially performed by a third-party consultant and then later brought in-house. The transition of the function to the bank generally occurs after appropriate staff have been hired or trained to conduct and interpret the analyses.

Regardless of whether your bank chooses to perform your analyses in-house or to outsource the process, it is an industry best practice to perform fair lending statistical analyses at the direction and under the supervision of legal counsel. Outside counsel with expertise in fair lending are well-positioned to provide insight on emerging enforcement trends, as well as evolving regulatory expectations, and industry best practices for fair lending monitoring programs. The use of outside counsel when conducting fair lending statistical analyses also provides greater protection in establishing and maintaining attorney-client privilege.

Although the CFPB and prudential regulators do not believe that the attorney-client privilege applies to statistical analyses in a supervisory or examination context, it is still advisable to conduct such analyses under attorney-client privilege to initially attempt to claim the privilege and/or protect the results from inadvertent disclosure to third parties, which could lead to litigation.

CHAPTER X.
WHAT TO DO IF YOUR BANK BECOMES THE TARGET OF A FAIR LENDING INVESTIGATION OR ENFORCEMENT ACTION

Fair lending investigations and enforcement actions can be lengthy, costly, and resource-intensive events for a bank. Where a regulator determines that the bank has violated a fair lending law, the matter may also result in significant reputational harm and multi-million dollar settlements. In the event of a threatened fair lending investigation or enforcement action, it is crucial that your bank respond quickly yet strategically.

A. How Fair Lending Investigations and Enforcement Actions Arise — and What to Expect

Typically, a fair lending investigation or enforcement action arises through the supervision and examination process. A prudential regulator (the OCC, FDIC, or FRB) or the CFPB may discover an issue through a consumer complaint or during an examination that it deems to be a violation of the federal fair lending laws. If the alleged violation of the federal fair lending laws is an isolated incident or is not deemed to be severe, it may simply be noted in a supervisory letter or indicated as a "Matter Requiring Attention" in an examination report. If the alleged violation is deemed severe and/or constitutes a pattern or practice of alleged discrimination, then it may lead to a preliminary supervisory determination and the issuance of a "15-day letter" by the prudential regulators or a Potential Action and Request for Response ("PARR") letter by the CFPB. A 15-

day letter or PARR letter is typically issued by the Washington headquarters office of the prudential regulator or CFPB.

Banks often discover the intent of an agency to pursue an enforcement action or a referral to the DOJ even before a 15-day letter or PARR letter is received through discussions with examiners while they are still on-site, at the "soft" exit meeting, or formal exit meeting. Bank management and the board of directors should make every effort to address and resolve any significant fair lending issues raised either during the exam or during the soft exit meeting before the examiners leave the bank's premises. If that approach fails, bank management should remain in communication with the examination team and attempt to resolve the issue before the official exit meeting or before the bank receives a 15-day letter or PARR letter. It is often helpful to enlist the assistance of the regulator's regional office staff to attempt to resolve the matter before a 15-day or PARR letter is issued because the regional office can help staff in the Washington office better understand the facts and the bank's position on the matter. By facilitating communication, the regional office can serve as a liaison between the bank and regulators in Washington, who are the ultimate decision makers on the matter.

Both the 15-day letter and PARR letter may provide the bank with notice of preliminary findings of a violation or violations of the federal fair lending laws. If there is a potential violation that could be referred to DOJ, then the 15-day letter or PARR letter provides the bank with notice of the potential for such a referral. The 15-day and PARR letters may also notify the bank that the regulator is considering taking supervisory action, such as a non-public memorandum of understanding or a public enforcement action, based on potential violations identified and described in the letter.

The bank is required to respond to the 15-day letter within that prescribed timeframe and, for the CFPB's PARR letter, within 14 days, although short extensions of time can often be negotiated with the regulator. The response must set forth any reasons of fact, law, or policy concerning why the regulator should not take action against the bank and provide supporting documentation, if appropriate. In some cases, the regulator will request additional documentation after reviewing the bank's response. The information provided by the bank is designed to help the regulator determine whether it is appropriate to take supervisory or enforcement action against the bank.

If your bank receives an unfavorable supervisory letter or fair lending examination report, it might foreshadow a forthcoming investigation or enforcement action and provide time for the bank to prepare accordingly. Alternatively, a regulator may issue a civil investigative demand ("CID"), which is designed to compel production of documents, responses to interrogatories, or testimony of witnesses prior to instituting any legal proceedings. A CID is often unanticipated and may be prompted by consumer complaints, advocacy groups, or whistleblowers; referrals from cooperating agencies; or other factors that fuel a regulator's sense that the bank has engaged in discriminatory practices.

If your bank first receives a CID, signaling the beginning of a regulatory investigation, it must act urgently. Under CFPB rules, for example, the bank must first "meet and confer" with investigators (to negotiate the CID's scope and the investigative process) within 10 days of service;[93] file a petition to amend or quash the CID within 20 days;[94] and produce the often-substantial amount of requested documents, testimony, responses to written questions, or other materials within the short amount of allotted time (generally 30 days).

B. Choosing the Right Defense Team

In light of these accelerated regulatory timelines, your bank must promptly determine the purpose and scope of the investigation and establish an appropriate response team to coordinate its defense. A lean fair lending response team might consist of the bank's general counsel, chief compliance (or fair lending) officer, chief information officer, relevant business executives, and potentially a third-party statistical consultant.[95] Other executives or employees may be added to the team as needed.

One of the first decisions your bank needs to make in response to a fair lending inquiry or investigation is whether to retain outside counsel or to respond to the issue through internal resources. This choice is an important one because experienced fair lending counsel may be able to facilitate a resolution through the supervisory process rather than the enforcement process, pursue a private informal enforcement action instead of a public enforcement action, or persuade the agency that no further action is necessary.

Fair lending counsel can also play a critical role in negotiations that the bank would prefer not to engage in itself insofar as the dialogue creates tension in the regulatory relationship between the bank and the agency. Outside counsel may also have working relationships with the regulators and enforcement agencies that will further your bank's credibility and help you navigate the process more effectively.

On the other hand, a bank may consider handling a fair lending matter in-house if it has experienced legal counsel with the subject matter expertise, skill set, and time to handle an investigation, which may involve extensive negotiations, interrogatories, written submissions, investigative hearings, and meetings with the regulators. Apart from the cost savings of using in-house counsel in a fair lending matter, certain efficiencies can be gained from the preexisting institutional knowledge of the bank's operations and supervisory history.

Some banks prefer to use in-house legal to retain greater control over the tone of the dialogue to ensure that discussions do not become overly adversarial or to avoid the appearance that they are "lawyering up." Each bank must factor the costs and benefits of using outside counsel to handle a fair lending matter, recognizing that all the risks of a seemingly innocuous inquiry are not always evident from the outset and only become apparent after some period of time.

C. Your Board Must Stay Apprised of the Proceedings

As with fair lending examinations, the board of directors typically is not involved in the day-to-day management of a significant fair lending compliance issue arising during an examination, a fair lending investigation, or an enforcement action. Bank directors, however, must understand the nature of the investigation and oversee the bank's enforcement defense, providing consultation when necessary.

The board (or a delegated committee) should always be made aware of any informal investigative request or threatened enforcement action, and it should request periodic updates from legal counsel on the status of the investigation. Many boards appoint at least one director to serve as a liaison between the board and the response team during an open investigation to ensure regular communication between management and the board and clear direction from the board on material decisions relating to the investigation.

D. What Is the Right Defense Strategy?

While legal counsel will advise your bank on recommended defense strategies as they become relevant, your bank and board should consider certain key issues in advance:

- *How cooperative will your bank be?* Cooperating with a regulator might foster a relationship of trust and credibility that pays off during current negotiations and future proceedings. However, being overly conciliatory can result in an adverse outcome for the bank that might have otherwise been avoided with an appropriate level of advocacy and dialogue. Refusal to cooperate is generally ill-advised insofar as it may foment distrust that results in a more aggressive investigation or enforcement action.

- *Will your bank make public a non-public proceeding?* While investigations are generally confidential, certain laws, particularly for publicly traded companies, may mandate public disclosure of enforcement proceedings. Likewise, if the bank petitions the CFPB to quash a CID, the investigation generally becomes public.[96] To the extent that public disclosure is discretionary, consider the resulting reputational harm (including anticipated media coverage, potential public relations efficacy, and employee morale) and the potential instigation of a parallel civil suit.

- *Should your bank prepare a response to a preliminary determination of a fair lending violation?* Toward the end of an examination or investigation, a fair lending regulator will notify a bank that it has made a preliminary determination of a fair lending violation and provide the bank with an opportunity to respond to the agency with additional facts or analysis that may alter their conclusion.[97] While banks may choose not to respond to an agency's letter indicating its preliminary determination of a violation, it is rarely in the bank's best interest to provide no response at all. To properly take advantage of this opportunity, many banks prepare a full legal and statistical analysis and, where appropriate, file reviews.

Ultimately, the best overarching strategy is for your bank to be strategic in its management of the investigation or examination and all related communications. Your response team knows and has better access to your bank than does a regulator, which must continuously adapt to the facts it gathers and analysis it develops throughout the investigation. The key is to think ahead and prepare to adapt your strategy to the facts and analysis as they develop.

E. Opportunity to Mitigate Risk

Your bank should treat a fair lending inquiry or investigation as an opportunity to mitigate future fair lending risk. For example, the bank should consider whether the risks identified in the prior matter flagged the need to reform bank policies or procedures or to conduct a fair lending risk assessment of relevant business units.

Alternatively, if employees are implicated as wrongdoers in an overt discrimination or disparate treatment matter, your bank should consider appropriate disciplinary and oversight actions that will prevent reoccurrence such as training or employee communications.

In addition, the board of directors should consider whether the prior fair lending matter identified areas where the board should expand its oversight of fair lending compliance, as discussed above in Chapter II.

APPENDIX A:
FAIR LENDING LAWS & REGULATIONS

This Appendix A provides a brief overview of two primary federal fair lending laws, ECOA and the FHA. Both ECOA and the FHA prohibit discrimination on specific bases. Some state and local fair lending laws may contain additional prohibited bases that are not discussed in this Handbook. This Appendix A also provides a brief overview of key federal laws that are related to fair lending, but are not fair lending laws *per se*.

A. Equal Credit Opportunity Act

ECOA, which is implemented by Regulation B, is enforced by the CFPB. ECOA was enacted in 1974 following hearings held by the National Commission on Consumer Finance in 1972, which demonstrated that women faced significant difficulties in attempting to obtain access to consumer credit. As a result, the focus of the original version of ECOA was on women, with the stated purpose of the law being to require financial institutions engaged in extending credit to make credit "equally available to all creditworthy customers *without regard to sex or marital status*."[98] Subsequent amendments to ECOA in 1976 added seven additional prohibited bases to the law.[99]

ECOA makes it unlawful for any creditor to discriminate against an applicant on a prohibited basis during any aspect of a credit transaction.[100] ECOA also makes it unlawful for any creditor to discourage a reasonable person from making or pursuing an application on a prohibited basis. The prohibited bases under ECOA are:

ECOA Prohibited Bases
  • Race • National Origin • Color • Religion • Sex • Age • Receipt of Public Assistance Income • Marital Status • A consumer's good faith exercise of any right under the Consumer Credit Protection Act

ECOA applies to both consumer and commercial credit and applies to the entire credit life cycle, from new product development and marketing through servicing, collections, and foreclosure or repossession. ECOA applies to both mortgage and non-mortgage products.

Regulation B imposes additional technical requirements that are intended to further the purpose of ECOA, including particular actions within the lending and servicing process that are prohibited, permitted, or required. Regulation B contains an Official Staff Commentary ("Commentary") that was originally issued by the FRB and subsequently adopted by the CFPB, which further interprets ECOA's requirements.[101] It is a good practice for your bank's legal and compliance staff to review the Commentary to further understand the requirements of Regulation B.

1. CFPB Guidance on Same-Sex Marriage

In response to the U.S. Supreme Court's 2013 decision in *United States v. Windsor*,[102] the CFPB issued guidance designed to ensure equal treatment for legally married same-sex couples.[103] In *Windsor*, the Court held as unconstitutional Section 3 of the Defense of Marriage Act, which defined the word "marriage" as "a legal union between one man and one woman as husband and wife" and the word "spouse" as referring "only to a person of the opposite sex who is a husband or a wife."[104]

The CFPB's guidance states that, regardless of a person's state of residency, the Bureau will consider a person who is married under the laws of any jurisdiction to be married nationwide for purposes of enforcing, administering, or interpreting the statutes, regulations, and policies under the Bureau's jurisdiction. The CFPB added that it "will not regard a person to be married by virtue of being in a domestic partnership, civil union, or other relationship not denominated by law as a marriage."[105]

2. ECOA Supervisory and Enforcement Authority

The CFPB has authority to promulgate rules under ECOA. The CFPB also has primary supervisory and enforcement authority for ECOA over banks with more than $10 billion in assets and non-banks that offer consumer loan products or services or engage in consumer lending. The prudential regulators — FRB, OCC, and the FDIC — have supervisory and enforcement authority for ECOA for banks with less than $10 billion in assets. The FTC has overlapping supervisory and enforcement authority for ECOA with the

CFPB over non-banks that offer consumer loan products or services.[106] DOJ conducts investigations of "pattern or practice" ECOA violations referred to it by the CFPB and prudential regulators, and it may also initiate its own investigations.

ECOA also provides for private rights of action, whereby individual plaintiffs may seek civil damages in individual or class action lawsuits.[107]

The CFPB may enforce certain ECOA violations on its own, but it must refer any matter to DOJ where the CFPB has reason to believe that one or more creditors has engaged in a "pattern or practice" of discouraging or denying applications for credit in violation of Section 701(a) of the ECOA (which contains ECOA's basic prohibition on discrimination) to DOJ.[108] The CFPB has primary authority to enforce ECOA against banks with more than $10 billion in assets. The CFPB has authority to commence a case in federal court if DOJ declines to pursue the referral or in cases that involve allegations other than discouraging or denying applications. The Dodd-Frank Act requires that the CFPB work together with the FTC,[109] HUD, and DOJ to coordinate enforcement activities and promote consistent regulatory treatment of consumer financial products and services.

Before the CFPB was established, a bank's prudential regulator was primarily responsible for investigating federal ECOA violations. Effective July 2011, the prudential regulators have supervisory and enforcement authority for ECOA only for banks with less than $10 billion in assets. The prudential regulators have back-up authority to enforce

ECOA for larger banks if the CFPB does not act on a referral from the regulator within 120 days.

Similar to the CFPB's authority under ECOA, a bank's prudential regulator is required to refer any "pattern or practice" violations of the ECOA to DOJ where the regulator has reason to believe that one or more creditors engaged in a pattern or practice of discouraging or denying applications for credit.[110] If DOJ declines to pursue the referral, then the prudential regulator can independently pursue its own ECOA enforcement action against a bank.

B. Fair Housing Act

The FHA was enacted in 1968 as Title VIII of the Civil Rights Act. The Civil Rights Act of 1968 was signed into law after a lengthy struggle in Congress to pass the legislation. President Lyndon Johnson used the national tragedy of Reverend Martin Luther King, Jr.'s assassination to finally urge Congress to approve the bill. President Johnson viewed the Civil Rights Act as a fitting memorial to Dr. King's life work, and he desired that the legislation be passed prior to Dr. King's funeral in Atlanta, Georgia. Congress passed the legislation, which included the FHA, only six days after Dr. King's death.

The purpose of the FHA is to prohibit discrimination in all aspects of the sale, rental, or financing of a dwelling (known as a "residential real estate-related transaction") on a prohibited basis. The prohibited bases under the FHA are:

FHA Prohibited Bases

- Race
- National Origin
- Color
- Religion
- Sex
- Handicap
- Familial Status (defined as children under the age of 18 living with a parent or legal custodian, pregnant women, and people securing custody of children under 18)

The FHA is primarily enforced by HUD, which maintains rulemaking authority, but the DOJ and the prudential regulators also share enforcement authority.[111] Each prudential regulator is required to forward any facts or information to HUD alleging violations of FHA that arise through receipt of a consumer complaint, an examination, or other means. If such facts or information indicate a possible pattern or practice of discrimination in violation of the FHA, then the prudential regulator must also forward the facts or information to DOJ.[112]

1. HUD's Equal Access and Disparate Impact Rules

In January 2012, HUD issued a final rule, which amended its regulations to prohibit discrimination based on actual or perceived sexual orientation or gender identity in regard to mortgage loans insured by the Federal Housing Administration.[113] To date, HUD has entered into one settlement with a national bank based on allegations that the bank denied a Federal Housing Administration loan to a lesbian couple.[114]

In February 2013, HUD issued a final rule that codifies the disparate impact theory — discussed further in Chapter III.[115]

2. FHA Enforcement and Supervisory Authority

HUD may pursue actions individually or work with the prudential regulators and the CFPB. A regulator must refer a matter to DOJ if it has evidence that a bank engaged in a possible pattern or practice of discrimination in violation of the FHA. On its own initiative, DOJ may also bring an action in federal court whenever it "has reasonable cause to believe that any person or group of persons is engaged in a pattern or practice" that violated the FHA or that "any group of persons has been denied any rights [under the FHA] and such denial raises an issue of general public importance."[116] The prudential regulators have supervisory and enforcement authority for enforcing the FHA for all banks.

An individual alleging FHA violations may file a complaint with HUD.[117] Upon the filing of a complaint, a HUD investigator will determine whether there is enough evidence to support an FHA claim. If there is sufficient evidence, the HUD investigator will give the parties an opportunity to pursue voluntary conciliation. If one or both parties refuse to conciliate, HUD conducts an investigation and determines whether there is probable cause to commence administrative proceedings. In addition to investigating individual consumer complaints, the HUD Secretary may initiate its own investigations.[118] HUD can either determine liability through its own administrative process or refer the matter to DOJ upon election of any party to the action. Complainants may also file a private suit on their own behalf.

C. Community Reinvestment Act

The CRA was enacted in 1977 to encourage banks to lend to the entire community from which banks drew deposits – specifically, to provide credit to residents of low- and moderate-income neighborhoods in their local communities. The CRA is not a fair lending law because it does not by itself prohibit discriminatory conduct based on race, ethnicity or membership in any other protected class, but it supports the objectives of the fair lending laws. The CRA is enforced by the prudential regulators, and those regulators issue rules implementing the CRA.

It is important to note that fair lending and CRA performance are linked in the examination process. The prudential regulators examine and rate a bank's compliance with the CRA. A bank that violates the fair lending laws and regulations can be subject to a CRA ratings downgrade by its examining agency and can face restrictions on its ability to engage in certain business activities, including opening a new branch or entering into a merger.

The CRA does not give government agencies or private individuals a statutory cause of action against banks. Nevertheless, the CRA has become increasingly tied to fair lending as regulators find fault with banks' long-standing self-designated assessment areas and use it as proof of discrimination in redlining enforcement actions. Private litigants have supported their fair lending claims by alleging that a bank failed to meet its CRA obligations.

D. Home Mortgage Disclosure Act

HMDA, which is implemented by Regulation C, requires certain mortgage lenders to collect and report to federal regulators, and disclose to the public, certain data about mortgage loan applications and originations, including the race, national origin and gender of loan applicants.[119] On an annual basis, lenders must disclose all of the information specified in Appendix A to Regulation C, commonly referred to as "HMDA data" to the appropriate government agency through the FFIEC, which then makes aggregate information for each lender available to the public (typically each September).

HMDA is also not a fair lending law, but government agencies use HMDA data as an initial screening mechanism for fair lending examinations to determine mortgage lending risk areas. Furthermore, federal regulators, consumer advocacy groups, and private litigants rely primarily on HMDA data when claiming that a bank did not apply its mortgage lending policies or practices equally to similarly situated applicants or borrowers. For instance, a plaintiff could develop a regression model using HMDA data to identify potential disparities in loan pricing for minority applicants and non-minority applicants.

It is important to recognize that HMDA data provide an incomplete – and potentially misleading – picture of a lender's underwriting and pricing practices. In an attempt to address this concern, the Dodd-Frank Act amends HMDA to require banks to collect and report additional information for mortgage home purchase and origination data, commonly referred to as "HMDA plus data."[120] In July 2014, the CFPB issued a proposed rule that would substantially expand the scope of HMDA data reporting requirements for mortgage lenders.[121]

On October 15, 2015, the CFPB issued a final rule which modifies some aspects of its proposal.[122] Data points to be reported under the final rule include: (i) additional information on applicants, borrowers, and the underwriting process, including age, credit score, debt-to-income ratio; (ii) additional information about the property securing the loan, such as property value and more detail on manufactured and multifamily housing; (iii) additional information on the features of the loan, such as pricing information, loan term, interest rate, introductory rate period, non-amortizing features, and the type of loan; and (iv) unique identifiers, including the property address, loan originator identifier, and a legal entity identifier for the financial institution. Most of the provisions of the final rule will take effect on January 1, 2018. Lenders will be required to collect the new data during 2018 and then report that data by March 1, 2019. The CFPB has not yet decided how much of the new information, some of which is highly sensitive, will be made publicly available.

The final rule also added a condition before a bank will be required to collect and report HMDA data. Under the current regulation, an institution must collect HMDA data for a given year if it (i) as of the preceding December 31, had assets above a threshold that is adjusted annually for inflation ($44 million in 2015[123]) and had a home or branch office in an MSA; (ii) in the preceding calendar year, originated at least one home purchase loan or refinancing of a home purchase loan that was secured by a first lien on a 1-4 family dwelling; (iii) meets one or more criterion related to federal or government-sponsored enterprise involvement with the loan, including being federally insured or regulated.[124]

The final rule also provides that, in order to be required to collect HMDA data in a given year, the bank must have originated at least 25 home purchase loans or refinancing of home purchase loans (including multi-family loans) in each of the preceding two calendar years. This new condition, which goes into effect for data collection efforts beginning on January 1, 2017, will allow additional banks with a low level of home loan activity to avoid reporting. The current HMDA rules will continue to apply to data collected during calendar year 2017.

In recent years, the federal regulators — and the CFPB in particular — have placed increased emphasis on the accuracy of HMDA data. During 2013, the CFPB brought enforcement actions against two banks for inaccurate HMDA data submissions and also issued regulatory guidance on HMDA.[125]

Regulation C contains an Official Staff Commentary (Supplement I to 12 C.F.R. Part 1003), issued by the FRB and subsequently adopted by the CFPB, which further interprets HMDA's requirements. Additional guidance on HMDA data collecting and reporting requirements can be found in "A Guide to HMDA Reporting: Getting It Right!"[126] See Chapter VIII and Appendix C for more information.

E. Unfair, Deceptive, and Abusive Acts or Practices

Over the past eight years, federal regulators, enforcement agencies and consumer advocacy groups have placed increasing focus on the need for banks to be more accountable for engaging in responsible lending. Responsible lending emphasizes economic and procedural fairness and transparency in dealing with consumers, including, among other things, providing clear, balanced and understandable terms and conditions, allowing consumers to make informed choices, refraining from taking unfair advantage of vulnerable consumer populations, and ensuring that financial products and services provide value to consumers commensurate with the costs.[127] Responsible lending is based primarily on violations of the Federal UDAP laws, section 5 of the FTC Act[128] and sections 1031 and 1036 of the Dodd-Frank Act,[129] but all 50 states and the District of Columbia have their own UDAP laws that can be enforced by the state attorney general and, in some instances, through a private right of action.

Although the FTC has enforced the federal UDAP statute for decades, a current hot topic is the "abusive" act or practice prohibited by the Dodd-Frank Act. Although the CFPB has authority under the Dodd-Frank Act to further define the concept by regulation, the CFPB has indicated in public statements by Director Richard Cordray and other officials that the Bureau intends to define the term on a case-by-case basis through enforcement actions.[130]

CFPB representatives have stated that a UDAAP may also violate other federal or state laws, and, based on public enforcement actions, the Bureau often alleges UDAAP violations where it finds a violation of other consumer financial protection laws.[131] As a result, it appears that the CFPB is using its UDAAP enforcement authority expansively.

Responsible banking laws — such as UDAAP — and fair lending often intersect because both concepts involve the unfair treatment of consumers. For example, an unclear disclosure about the fees charged for a particular loan may disproportionately affect members of a protected class and result in substantial injury to affected consumers.

In light of these developments, as you oversee your bank's fair lending program in your role as a bank director, consider whether it may be appropriate to expand the scope of your institution's program to include responsible lending concepts — in other words, a "fair and responsible lending" program.

APPENDIX B:
REGULATORY REFERENCE MATERIALS

Regulatory Guidance
Key Fair Lending Regulatory Guidance

- Interagency Policy Statement on Discrimination in Lending, 59 Fed. Reg. 18267 (Apr. 15, 1994)
- FDIC FIL 36-96 – Side-by-Side: A Guide to Fair Lending (June 6, 1996)
- OCC Bulletin 2011-39, *Fair Credit Reporting and Equal Credit Opportunity Acts – Risk-Based Pricing Notices – Final Rules* (Sept. 22, 2011)
- OCC Bulletin 2011-41, *Community Reinvestment Act Notices, Fair Housing Act Posters, Equal Credit Opportunity Act Notices – Guidance* (Oct. 11, 2011)
- CFPB Bulletin 2012-04 (Fair Lending), *Lending Discrimination* (April 18, 2012)
- CFPB Bulletin 2013-02, *Indirect Auto Lending and Compliance with the Equal Credit Opportunity Act* (Mar. 21, 2013)
- VA Circular 26-13-18, *Interim Process for Determining Spousal Income Qualifications in Jurisdictions that Recognize Same-Sex Marriage* (Sept. 26, 2013)
- *Memorandum on Implementation of United States v. Windsor* from Attorney General Eric Holder to the President dated June 20, 2014
- *Memorandum on Ensuring Equal Treatment for Same-Sex Married Couples* from CFPB Director Richard Cordray to CFPB Staff dated June 25, 2014
- CFPB, *Using Publicly Available Information to Proxy for Unidentified Race and Ethnicity* (Summer 2014)

Key HMDA Regulatory Guidance

- OCC Bulletin 2009-2, *Home Mortgage Disclosure Act – Rate Spread Reporting Threshold under Regulation C* (Jan. 5, 2009)
- OCC Bulletin 2011-5, *Home Mortgage Disclosure Act – Exemption Threshold for Depository Institutions Under Regulation C* (Jan. 26, 2011)
- OCC Bulletin 2013-5, *Home Mortgage Disclosure Act – Consumer Financial Protection Bureau Final Rule for Reporting Thresholds* (Feb. 6, 2013)
- CFPB Bulletin 2013-11, *Home Mortgage Disclosure Act (HMDA) and Regulation C – Compliance Management; CFPB HMDA Resubmission Schedule and Guidelines; and HMDA Enforcement* (Oct. 9, 2013)
- FFIEC – *A Guide to HMDA Reporting: Getting it Right!* (2013)

Key Responsible Lending Guidance

- OCC Advisory Letter 2002-3, *Guidance on Unfair and Deceptive Acts or Practices* (Mar. 22, 2002)
- OCC Bulletin 2003-1, *Credit Card Lending – Account Management and Loss Allowance Guidance* (Jan. 8, 2003)
- OCC Advisory Letter 2003-2, *Guidelines for National Banks to Guard Against Predatory and Abusive Lending Practices* (Feb. 21, 2003)
- OCC Advisory Letter 2003-3, *Avoiding Predatory and Abusive Lending Practices in Brokered and Purchased Loans* (Feb. 21, 2003)
- FRB and FDIC, *Unfair or Deceptive Acts or Practices by State-Chartered Banks* (Mar. 11, 2004)
- OCC Advisory Letter 2004-4, *Secured Credit Cards* (Apr. 28, 2004)
- OCC Advisory Letter 2004-10, *Credit Card Practices* (Sept. 14, 2004)

- OCC Bulletin 2005-3, *Guidelines Establishing Standards for Residential Mortgage Lending Practices, Appendix C to 12 C.F.R. Part 30* (Feb. 2, 2005)
- *Joint Guidance on Overdraft Protection Programs,* 70 Fed. Reg. 9127 (Feb. 24, 2005)
- OCC Bulletin 2010-15, *Overdraft Protection: Opt-In Requirements and Related Marketing Issues* (Apr. 12, 2010)
- FDIC FIL-81-2010, *Overdraft Payment Programs and Consumer Protection Final Overdraft Payment Supervisory Guidance* (Nov. 24, 2010)
- CFPB Bulletin 2013-07, *Prohibition of Unfair, Deceptive, or Abusive Acts or Practices in the Collection of Consumer Debts* (July 10, 2013)
- FFIEC, *Interagency Guidance Regarding Unfair or Deceptive Credit Practices* (Aug. 22, 2014

Key CRA Regulatory Guidance

- OCC Bulletin 2011-41, *Community Reinvestment Act Notices, Fair Housing Act Posters, Equal Credit Opportunity Act Notices – Guidance* (Oct. 11, 2011)
- OCC Bulletin 2012-20, *Community Reinvestment Act – List of Distressed or Underserved Nonmetropolitan Middle-Income Geographies* (July 30, 2012)
- OCC Bulletin 2012-29, *Community Reinvestment Act – Income Level for Median Family Income* (Sept. 24, 2012)
- OCC Bulletin 2013-3, *Compliance: Community Reinvestment Act – Small and Intermediate Small Bank and Savings Association Asset Thresholds Regulatory Revision* (Jan. 25, 2013)
- OCC, FRB, and FDIC, *Community Reinvestment Act; Interagency Questions and Answers Regarding Community Reinvestment; Notice,* 78 Fed. Reg. 69671 (Nov. 20, 2013)

Examination Procedures

Fair Lending Examination Procedures

- FRB Consumer Compliance Handbook, V. Federal Fair Lending Regulations and Statutes (Jan. 2006)
- FFIEC Interagency Fair Lending Examination Procedures (Aug. 2009)
- OCC Comptroller's Handbook – Fair Lending (Jan. 2010)
- CFPB Supervision and Examination Manual – Equal Credit Opportunity Act (ECOA) Procedures (June 4, 2013)
- CFPB Supervision and Examination Manual – Equal Credit Opportunity Act (ECOA) Baseline Review Procedures (July 19, 2013)
- FDIC Compliance Examination Manual, IV. Fair Lending Laws and Regulations (June 2014)

HMDA Examination Procedures

- OCC Comptroller's Handbook – Home Mortgage Disclosure (Feb. 2010)
- CFPB Supervision and Examination Manual – Home Mortgage Disclosure Act (Oct. 2012)

Responsible Lending (UDAP/UDAAP) Examination Procedures

- FRB Consumer Compliance Handbook, IV. Regulation AA: Unfair or Deceptive Acts or Practices: Credit Practices Rule (Jan. 2006) & Federal Trade Commission Act Section 5: Unfair or Deceptive Acts or Practices (June 2008)
- CFPB Supervision and Examination Manual – Unfair, Deceptive, or Abusive Acts or Practices (Oct. 2012)
- FDIC Compliance Examination Manual, VII. Abusive Practices (June 2014)

CRA Examination Procedures
• FRB Consumer Compliance Handbook, VI. Community Reinvestment Act (June 2007)
• Intermediate Small Institution CRA Examination Procedures OCC, FRB, FDIC and OTS (July 2007)
• Small Institution CRA Examination Procedures OCC, FRB, FDIC and OTS (July 2007)
• Strategic Plan CRA Examination Procedures OCC, FRB, FDIC and OTS (July 2007)
• Wholesale/Limited Purpose CRA Examination Procedures OCC, FRB, FDIC and OTS (July 2007)
• FDIC Compliance Examination Manual, XI. Community Reinvestment Act (June 2011)
• Large Institution CRA Examination Procedures OCC, FRB, and FDIC (Apr. 2014)

APPENDIX C:
CURRENT AND NEW HMDA REPORTING REQUIREMENTS

Current HMDA Reporting Requirements (Applicable to Data Collection through December 31, 2017)

Loan Information

- Loan identification number
- Date of application
- Type of loan
- Purpose of loan
- Whether application is a request for preapproval and whether it resulted in denial or origination
- Amount of the loan or the amount applied for
- Type of action taken and date of action
- Whether the loan is subject to the Home Ownership and Equity Protection Act (HOEPA)
- Lien status of the loan (first lien, subordinate lien or not secured by a lien on a dwelling)
- Spread between the annual percentage rate (APR) and the applicable prime offer rate if the spread is equal to or greater than 1.5 percentage points for first lien loans or 3.5 percentage points for subordinate lien loans
- Purchaser of the loan (if it is sold in the same year the loan is purchased or originated)

Property Information

- Property type (manufactured housing, multifamily dwelling, 1-to-4 family dwelling other than manufactured housing)
- Owner-occupancy status of the property
- Location of property by MSA, state, county and census tract

Applicant Information
• Ethnicity, race and sex of the applicant(s) or borrower(s) (optional for loans purchased by financial institutions)   • Gross annual income relied on in processing the application (optional for loans purchased by financial institutions)   • Number of applicants
Other Optional Data
• Reason for denial   • Requests for preapproval that are approved but not accepted by applicant   • Home equity lines of credit made in whole or in part for the purpose of home improvement or home purchase

New HMDA Reporting Requirements   (Application to Data Collection Beginning January 1, 2018)
Expanded Product and Reporting Coverage
• Open-end lines of credit, including home-equity lines of credit (HELOC) (regardless of purpose) for which reporting was previously optional   • Home-equity loans falling under the definition of "closed-end mortgage loan"   • Preapproval requests that were approved, but not accepted   • Reverse mortgages (previously not required if they were reportable transactions)   • Loans not secured by a dwelling are no longer reported
Loan and Fee Information

• Application channel – whether it was a direct application and was or	• Interest rate • Loan term • Non-amortizing features

would be initially payable to the institution

- Universal loan identifier (ULI) in a specified format – may not identify an individual customer
- Difference between APR and "average prime offer ate" (market rate) on all loans (not just loans above a higher-cost threshold)
- Balloon payment
- Borrower-paid loan costs and origination charges
- Discount points
- HELOC flag
- HELOC or open-end reverse mortgage first draw amount (if made upon account opening)
- Introductory rate period
- Interest only payments

(balloon payments, interest-only, negative amortization, etc.)

- Pre-payment penalty
- Purpose of loan includes new "cash-out refinancing" and "other" categories
- Qualified Mortgage (QM) flag
- Reverse mortgage flag
- Total discount points
- Total origination charges
- Total points and fees

Property Information

- Combined loan-to-value (CLTV) ratio
- Construction method

- Number of units on the property
- Property postal address

(site-built or manufactured housing) • Whether manufactured home land is owned or leased • Multifamily affordable units	• Property value (sales or appraised value) • Total units (number of individual dwelling units securing the loan) • Use of property (principal residence, second residence, or investment property)

Applicant Information

• Age (applicant and co-applicant) • Credit score (applicant and co-applicant)	• Debt-to-income (DTI) ratio

Other Information

- Automated underwriting system (AUS) used and system recommendation
- Credit score provider (applicant and co-applicant)
- Mortgage loan originator identifier (Nationwide Mortgage Licensing System and Registry unique identifier (NMLSR ID) – if multiple originators, report NMLSR ID for originator with primary responsibility for the transaction)
- Reason(s) for denial, indicating up to three (previously optional except for certain OCC- and FDIC-supervised institutions, now required for all applications)

About the Authors

David Baris, a partner in the Washington, D.C. office of BuckleySandler LLP, represents financial institutions throughout the United States on securities, corporate, transactional, and regulatory matters. Mr. Baris has spent more than 30 years in practice assisting financial institutions in critical and transformative business changes, including mergers, acquisitions, tender offers, holding company formations, going private transactions, securities offerings, proxy contests, and new product development. as well as more routine matters, such as periodic reporting and securities disclosure, Sarbanes-Oxley Act compliance, compliance with corporate governance listing requirements of the national securities exchanges, regulatory reporting and applications, executive compensation arrangements, employment agreements, and vendor management.

Mr. Baris also assists banks with regulatory examinations and represents them in negotiations of orders and enforcement actions instituted by regulatory agencies.

Before joining BuckleySandler, Mr. Baris was a partner of Kennedy & Baris LLP, which he founded in 1987. Mr. Baris brings to his practice experience as both a bank regulator and Congressional staffer, serving as Regional Counsel to the Comptroller of the Currency from 1977 to 1983 and Counsel to the Government Operations Committee, U.S. House of Representatives from 1972 to 1974.

Mr. Baris is the President of the American Association of Bank Directors (AABD). AABD provides bank directors with the resources with which to serve their institutions effectively and in a manner that will minimize risk of personal liability, and represents their interests before federal and state legislative bodies, banking supervisory agencies and judicial bodies. He is also a member of the General Counsel Advisory Group of the Independent Community Bankers of America. In 2013, he was appointed to the Federal Bar Association Banking Law Executive Council. From 2000 to 2004, Mr. Baris was a director of Mutual of Omaha Insurance Company and United of Omaha Life Insurance Company, a Fortune 500 company, serving on their Executive, Audit, and Investment Committees.

Mr. Baris writes and lectures widely on banking subjects.

Andrea K. Mitchell, a partner in the Washington, D.C. office of BuckleySandler LLP, focuses her practice on fair and responsible financial services. She advises financial services companies throughout the country in administrative enforcement and regulatory compliance matters involving fair lending, disparate impact, UDAAP, and other unfair, predatory, or anti-discrimination statutes and regulations. Ms. Mitchell represents clients in federal and state enforcement agency examinations and investigations, congressional investigations, and corporate internal investigations. Specifically, she has represented clients in examinations and investigations by the Department of Justice, Consumer Financial Protection Bureau, Federal Reserve Board, Office of the Comptroller of the Currency, Federal Deposit Insurance Corporation, Federal Trade Commission, Department of Housing and Urban Development, and State attorneys general.

Ms. Mitchell also has extensive experience in counseling banks and finance companies on regulatory compliance and risk management with respect to the Equal Credit Opportunity Act, Fair Housing Act, Truth in Lending Act, Truth in Savings Act, Fair Credit Reporting Act, and UDAAP laws.

Given recent areas of fair lending, fair servicing and UDAAP focus by the CFPB and the prudential regulators, Ms. Mitchell is actively advising her financial services clients on matters involving compliance and risk management, including:

- Pricing and underwriting discrimination
- Steering
- Redlining
- Product development
- Ancillary products
- Sales and marketing
- Servicing, collections, and loss mitigation activities
- Credit reporting
- Vendor management
- Claims fulfillment

Ms. Mitchell is a frequent speaker at conferences and seminars on fair lending, UDAAP, and CFPB topics and was a contributor to the American Bankers Association's Fair Lending Toolbox released in 2012. She also conducts in-house training and continuing legal education seminars on a variety of consumer compliance topics.

Prior to joining BuckleySandler, Ms. Mitchell served as a counsel in the Legal Division at the Federal Reserve Board.

While there, she worked on numerous consumer regulations, advised supervised entities on queries related to consumer protection statutes, and participated in several interagency task forces.

Ms. Mitchell was a litigation associate at Skadden, Arps, Slate, Meagher & Flom LLP before working at the Federal Reserve Board, and she served as a law clerk to the Honorable Mary Ellen Barbera of the Maryland Court of Special Appeals. She received her J.D. from American University (*summa cum laude*) in 2002 and her B.A. from the University of Wisconsin-Madison in 1993.

Lori J. Sommerfield, senior counsel in the Washington, D.C. office of BuckleySandler LLP, practices consumer financial protection law, with an emphasis on fair and responsible lending regulatory compliance and CFPB matters. Ms. Sommerfield brings to her practice over 25 years of experience in financial institutions law and compliance risk management, including leading one of the nation's largest bank's fair and responsible lending programs, serving as in-house counsel at two other major lenders, and working as a staff attorney at the FDIC.

Ms. Sommerfield practices extensively in the areas of fair and responsible banking (including the Equal Credit Opportunity Act, the Fair Housing Act, and unfair, deceptive or abusive acts or practices laws), and assists both banks and non-banks in preparing for and managing compliance examinations by the CFPB and federal prudential regulators. She also assists clients in defending fair lending investigations and potential enforcement actions.

Prior to joining BuckleySandler, Ms. Sommerfield managed Wells Fargo & Company's Corporate Fair & Responsible Lending Compliance Program, providing oversight for 18 consumer and non-consumer credit businesses. Ms. Sommerfield worked at Wells Fargo for five years and also served as Vice President and Compliance Manager for the Home & Consumer Finance Group's Fair & Responsible Lending Compliance Program, managing fair and responsible lending risks for several key lending businesses, including Wells Fargo Home Mortgage.

Ms. Sommerfield began her career as a staff attorney at the FDIC in Washington, D.C., where she worked in the Regulation & Legislation Section of the Legal Division developing banking policy and regulations. Subsequently, she served as Associate Counsel for Banking & Trust at ReliaStar Financial Corporation, a unitary thrift holding company, and Assistant General Counsel of ING DIRECT, the internet banking subsidiary of ING. Prior to joining Wells Fargo in 2004, Ms. Sommerfield was part of the financial institutions practice group at a Minneapolis law firm.

Ms. Sommerfield received her J.D. from the Catholic University of America's Columbus School of Law with a concentration in law and public policy. Ms. Sommerfield received a B.A. in Psychology from the University of Minnesota.

Shara M. Chang is Product Counsel for Affirm, Inc., a next generation financial services company offering consumer credit at the point of sale. Ms. Chang was previously an associate in the Washington, D.C. office of BuckleySandler LLP, where she represented corporate clients in connection with matters relating to consumer protection regulation and enforcement. Her practice focused on providing compliance advice relating to consumer protection laws as applied to a host of industries, including matters related to unfair, deceptive, and/or abusive acts or practices laws, Consumer Financial Protection Act, Equal Credit Opportunity Act, Fair Credit Reporting Act, Fair Housing Act, Real Estate Settlement Procedures Act, and the Truth in Lending Act.

Prior to joining BuckleySandler, Ms. Chang was an associate at Cleary Gottlieb Steen & Hamilton LLP, where her practice focused on U.S. bank regulatory matters, including regulatory aspects of bank mergers and acquisitions, bank charter formations and conversions, capital adequacy, and U.S. regulatory reform legislation.

Ms. Chang has been featured in the Lawyers of Color's 2013 Hot List Issue, which recognizes early to mid-year attorneys who are excelling in the legal profession. Ms. Chang has twice been recognized by Washington, D.C. *Super Lawyers* as a rising star in the areas of consumer law and banking. She was also honored by the National Bar Association with the "40 Under 40" Nation's Best Advocates Award.

Ms. Chang is active in the American Bar Association, where she was selected by the Business Law Section to serve as one of five Ambassadors nationwide from 2013-2015. She serves as Vice-Chair of the Consumer Financial Services Committee's Task Force on Diversity and Inclusion. Ms. Chang is the immediate Past President of the Greater Washington Area Chapter, Women Lawyers Division of the

National Bar Association (GWAC) and participated in the inaugural class of the D.C. Bar's Leadership Academy. She also serves as an Associate Trustee for the Washington Lawyers' Committee for Civil Rights and Urban Affairs.

Ms. Chang received her J.D. from Howard University (cum laude). During law school, she served as executive publications editor for the Howard Law Journal and interned for the Honorable Anna Blackburne-Rigsby of the District of Columbia Court of Appeals. Ms. Chang holds a M.A. in Economics from York University and a B.Com. from Ryerson University.

Endnotes

1   12 U.S.C. § 5481(13).

2   In the past, responsible lending largely focused on compliance with unfair or deceptive acts or practices law under Section 5 of the Federal Trade Commission Act ("FTC Act"), state anti-predatory lending laws, and the Home Ownership and Equity Protection Act ("HOEPA"), which places limits on high-cost mortgage loans. In recent years, responsible lending laws have been expanded to include unfair, deceptive, or abusive lending laws under the Dodd-Frank Act and the Servicemembers Civil Relief Act ("SCRA"). Responsible lending is often viewed as a complementary concept to fair lending, but it is only addressed tangentially in this book.

3   U.S. DEP'T OF JUSTICE, ATTORNEY GENERAL'S 2014 ANNUAL REPORT TO CONGRESS PURSUANT TO THE EQUAL CREDIT OPPORTUNITY ACT AMENDMENTS OF 1976 1 (2015).

4   Consent Order, United States v. Countrywide Fin. Corp., No. 2:11-cv-10540-PSG-AJW (C.D. Cal. Dec. 28, 2011).

5   Consent Order, United States v. Wells Fargo Bank, NA, No. 1:12-cv-01150-JDB (D.D.C. Sept. 21, 2012).

6   *See* Ally Financial Inc.; & Ally Bank, CFPB No. 2013-CFPB-0010 (Dec. 20, 2013) [hereinafter CFPB Ally Consent Order]. Creditors are prohibited under Regulation B from inquiring about a borrower's race, ethnicity, or gender in connection with non-mortgage loan applications. The federal government has adopted various methodologies to predict a person's race or ethnicity in non-mortgage lending investigations in order to determine which borrowers are prohibited basis group members.

7   In the event that an auto dealer charges the consumer an interest rate that is higher than the lender's buy rate, the lender may pay the auto dealer what is typically referred to as dealer "reserve" or "participation" — compensation based upon the difference in interest revenues between the buy rate and the actual note rate charged to the consumer in the retail installment contract executed with the dealer, or a percentage of that difference where the dealer and lender split the amount (*e.g.*, 50/50, 60/40, etc.). Dealer reserve is one method indirect auto lenders use to compensate dealers for the value they add by originating loans and

finding financing sources. The exact computation of compensation based on dealer mark-up varies across lenders and may even vary among programs at the same lender.

[8]   Consent Order, United States v. Synchrony Bank, No. 2:14-CV-00454-DS (D. Utah June 27, 2014); Synchrony Bank, f/k/a GE Capital Retail Bank, CFPB No. 2014-CFPB-0007 (June 19, 2014) [hereinafter CFPB Synchrony Bank Consent Order].

[9]   Agreed Order, United States v. Luther Burbank Sav., No. 2:12-cv-07809-JAK-FMO (C.D. Cal. Oct. 12, 2012).

[10]   Cmty. First Bank, No. AA-EC-2012-124, OCC No. 2013-025 (Mar. 18, 2013).

[11]   268 F.R.D. 627 (N.D. Cal. 2010).

[12]   *See* NAT'L FAIR HOUS. ALLIANCE, ZIP CODE INEQUALITY: DISCRIMINATION BY BANKS IN THE MAINTENANCE OF HOMES IN NEIGHBORHOODS OF COLOR (2014); NAT'L FAIR HOUS. ALLIANCE, THE BANKS ARE BACK – OUR NEIGHBORHOODS ARE NOT: DISCRIMINATION IN THE MAINTENANCE AND MARKETING OF REO PROPERTIES (2012); NAT'L FAIR HOUS. ALLIANCE, HERE COMES THE BANK, THERE GOES THE NEIGHBORHOOD (2011).

[13]   Conciliation Agreement, between U.S. Dep't of Hous. & Urban Dev. and Wells Fargo Bank, N.A., HUD No. 00-13-001-8 (June 5, 2013).

[14]   Press Release, Nat'l Fair Hous. Alliance, Mortgage Giant Fannie Mae Accused of Racial Discrimination in 34 U.S. Metro Areas (May 13, 2015).

[15]   *See, e.g.,* Press Release, Nat'l Fair Hous. Alliance, Bank of America Charged with Creating Unhealthy Housing Through Widespread Practice of Housing Discrimination (Nov. 14, 2013); Press Release, Nat'l Fair Hous. Alliance, U.S. Bank Accused of Racial Discrimination in Five More Cities (Nov. 18, 2014); Press Release, Nat'l Fair Hous. Alliance, Fannie Mae Contractor Accused of Race Discrimination in Four U.S. Cities (July 22, 2014). HUD found no violation by U.S. Bank and closed the matter in Jan. 2016, but apparently NFHA intends to appeal.

[16]   *See, e.g.,* Complaint, City of Miami v. JPMorgan Chase & Co., No. 1:14-cv-22205, 2014 WL 2709434 (S.D. Fla. June 13, 2014); First Amended Complaint, City of Los Angeles v. JPMorgan Chase & Co., No. 2:14-cv-04168, 2014 WL 4383509 (C.D. Cal. Aug. 26, 2014); Complaint, City of Miami v. Wells Fargo & Co., No. 1:13-cv-24508 (S.D. Fla. Dec. 13, 2013); Complaint, City of Miami v. Citigroup Inc., No. 1:13-cv-24510 (S.D. Fla. Dec. 13, 2013); Complaint, City of Miami Gardens v. Wells Fargo & Co., No. 1:14-cv-22203 (S.D. Fla. June 13, 2014); Complaint, City of Miami Gardens v. Citigroup Inc., No. 1:14-cv-22204(S.D. Fla. June 13, 2014); Complaint, City of Miami Gardens v. JPMorgan Chase & Co., No. 1:14-cv-22206 (S.D. Fla. June 13, 2014); Complaint, City of Miami Gardens v. Bank of Am. Corp., No. 1:14-cv-22202 (S.D. Fla. June 13, 2014); Complaint, City of Los Angeles v. Bank of America Corp., No. 2:13CV09046, 2013 WL 6502834 (C.D. Cal. Dec. 6, 2013); Complaint, City of Los Angeles v. Wells Fargo & Co., No. 2:13CV09007, 2013 WL 6916826 (C.D. Cal. Dec. 5, 2013); Complaint, City of Los Angeles v. Citigroup Inc., No. 2:13CV09009 (C.D. Cal. Dec. 5, 2013); Complaint, City of Oakland v. Wells Fargo & Co., No. 3:15-cv-04321 (N.D. Cal. Sept. 21, 2015); Complaint, DeKalb Cty. v. HSBC N. Am. Holdings Inc., No. 1:12-cv-03640 (N.D. Ga. Oct. 18, 2012); Amended Complaint, County of Cook v. HSBC North America Holdings Inc., No. 1:14-cv-2031, 2014 WL 1677060 (N.D. Ill. Mar. 31, 2014).

[17]   *See* U.S. DEP'T OF JUSTICE, *supra* note 3, at 18.

[18]   A "pattern or practice" of lending discrimination has not been clearly defined but has been addressed in regulatory guidance and judicial decisions. For example, the Interagency Policy Statement on Discrimination in Lending adopted by the federal banking agencies, DOJ, HUD, and other agencies declared that "[i]solated, unrelated or accidental occurrences will not constitute a pattern or practice" of discrimination, and conceded that "more than one [instance of discrimination] does not necessary constitute a pattern or practice." 59 Fed. Reg. 18,267, 18,271 (Apr. 15, 1994). The 1994 Interagency Statement maintains that "[t]he totality of the circumstances must be considered when assessing whether a pattern or practice is present." *Id.* Similarly, one seminal case found that for purposes of establishing pattern or practice, DOJ must establish "more than the mere occurrence of isolated or 'accidental' or sporadic discriminatory acts" and must show that

discrimination was the "standard operating procedure[,] the regulator rather than the usual practice." Int'l Brotherhood of Teamsters v. United States, 431 U.S. 324, 336 (1977).

[19] FED. FIN. INSTS. EXAMINATION COUNCIL, INTERAGENCY FAIR LENDING EXAMINATION PROCEDURES iv (2009).

[20] 24 C.F.R. § 100.500(c)(2).

[21] HUD's disparate impact rule already has been challenged in federal court. On November 4, 2014, the United States District Court for the District of Columbia vacated HUD's disparate impact rule and held that "the FHA prohibits disparate treatment *only*," and therefore HUD, in promulgating the disparate impact rule, "exceeded [its] authority under the [Administrative Procedures Act]." Am. Ins. Ass'n v. U.S. Dep't of Hous. & Urban Dev., 74 F. Supp. 3d 30, 31 (D.D.C. 2014). This case came on the heels of a case in the United States District Court of the Northern District of Illinois which held that "HUD's response to the insurance industry's concerns [regarding the disparate impact rule] was arbitrary and capricious." Property Cas. Insurers of Am. v. Donovan, 66 F. Supp. 3d 1018, 1051 (N.D. Ill. 2014). The court sent this matter back to HUD "for further explanation." *Id.*

[22] 135 S. Ct. 2507 (2011).

[23] It is important to note that the U.S. Supreme Court's opinion in *Inclusive Communities* did not specifically dictate the standards and burdens of proof that apply to the burden-shifting test in disparate impact claims. However, the Court's opinion emphasized proper limitations on the use of disparate impact to avoid serious constitutional questions and to protect defendants against "abusive" disparate impact claims. Tex. Dep't of Hous. & Cmty. Affairs v. Inclusive Cmtys. Project, Inc., 135 S. Ct. 2507, 2511 (2011).

With regard to the first step of the burden-shifting framework, the Court reaffirmed the significant burden on the plaintiff in establishing a *prima facie* case. The Court stated that a "robust causality requirement" is important, and that plaintiffs relying on a statistical disparity must show that a specific policy of defendant caused the disparity. *Id.* In the second step, in which the burden shifts to the defendant to refute the allegation, the Court determined that defendants in disparate impact cases must be given an opportunity to state and explain the valid interests served by their policies, and that those policies should be allowed if the defendants can demonstrate they are necessary to achieve a legitimate objective. Citing the seminal case of *Griggs v. Duke Power*, the Court stated that policies are not contrary to the disparate impact requirement unless they are "artificial, arbitrary, and unnecessary barriers." 401 U.S. 424, 431 (1971). In the third step, the Court indicated that before a business justification can be rejected, the plaintiff must show that there is "an available alternative . . . practice that has less disparate impact and services the [entity's] legitimate needs." Inclusive Cmtys., 135 S. Ct. at 2511 (quoting Ricci v. DeStefano, 557 U.S. 557, 578 (2009)). Finally, the Court noted that when courts do find liability under a disparate impact theory, their remedial orders should concentrate on the elimination of the practice.

24   Consent Order, United States v. Cmty. State Bank, No. 1:13-cv-10142 (E.D. Mi. Mar. 12, 2013).

25   Settlement Agreement, United States v. Citizens Republic Bancorp, Inc., No. 2:11-cv-11976 (E.D. Mich. June 23, 2011).

26   Agreed Order, United States v. Midwest BankCentre, No. 4:11-cv-01086-FRB (E.D. Mo. June 28, 2013).

27   Settlement Agreement, People v. Evans Bancorp, Inc., No. 14-cv-00726 (W.D.N.Y. Sept. 10, 2014).

28   Press Release, N.Y. Att'y Gen. Eric T. Schneiderman, A.G. Schneiderman Secures Agreement With Evans Bank Ending Discriminatory Mortgage Redlining in Buffalo (Sept. 10, 2015); *see also* Jessica Silver-Greenberg, *New York Accuses Evans Bank of Redlining*, N.Y. TIMES, Sept. 2, 2014, http://dealbook.nytimes.com/2014/09/02/new-york-set-to-accuse-evans-bank-of-redlining/?_r=0.

29   *See supra* note 16.

30   Consent Decree, United States v. Auto Fare, Inc., No. 3:14-cv-00008 (W.D.N.C. Feb. 10, 2015).

31   Complaint, Fair Hous. Justice Ctr. v. M&T Bank Corp., No. 15-cv-779 (S.D.N.Y. Feb. 3, 2014).

32   CFPB Synchrony Bank Consent Order, *supra* note 8.

33   Consent Order, United States v. AIG Fed. Sav. Bank, 1:10-cv-00178

(D. Del. Mar. 19, 2010).

[34]   Consent Order, Consumer Fin. Prot. Bureau v. Nat'l City Bank, No. 2:13-cv-01817 (W.D. Penn. Jan. 9, 2014).

[35]   *See, e.g.*, Press Release, Dep't of Justice, Justice Department Reaches Fair Lending Settlement with Chevy Chase Bank Resulting in $2.85 Million in Relief for Homeowners (Sept. 30, 2013); Press Release, Dep't of Justice, Justice Department Reaches Settlement with Southport Bank to Resolve Allegations of Mortgage Lending Discrimination (Sept. 26, 2013).

[36]   Conciliation Agreement, between U.S. Dep't of Hous. & Urban Dev. and Greenlight Fin. Servs., FHEO No. 09-13-0147-8 (July 1, 2014).

[37]   CONSUMER FIN. PROT. BUREAU ET AL., INTERAGENCY STATEMENT ON FAIR LENDING COMPLIANCE AND THE ABILITY-TO-REPAY AND QUALIFIED MORTGAGE STANDARDS RULE (2013).

[38]   *Id.* at 2-3

[39]   CONSUMER FIN. PROT. BUREAU, FAIR LENDING REPORT OF THE CONSUMER FINANCIAL PROTECTION BUREAU 10 (2015) [hereinafter CFPB 2015 Fair Lending Report]; CONSUMER FIN. PROT. BUREAU, FAIR LENDING REPORT OF THE CONSUMER FINANCIAL PROTECTION BUREAU 10 (2014) [hereinafter CFPB 2014 Fair Lending Report].

[40]   *See* Press Release, Consumer Fin. Prot. Bureau, Consumer Financial Protection Bureau Proposes New Federal Oversight of Nonbank Auto Finance Companies (Sept. 17, 2014); Defining Larger Participants of the Automobile Financing Market and Defining Certain Automobile Leasing Activity as a Financial Product or Service, 79 Fed. Reg. 60,762 (proposed Oct. 8, 2014); CONSUMER FIN. PROT. BUREAU, SUPERVISORY HIGHLIGHTS (2014); CONSUMER FIN. PROT. BUREAU, USING PUBLICLY AVAILABLE INFORMATION TO PROXY FOR UNIDENTIFIED RACE AND ETHNICITY: A METHODOLOGY AND ASSESSMENT (2014) [hereinafter CFPB White Paper].

[41]   CONSUMER FIN. PROT. BUREAU, CFPB BULL. NO. 2013-02, INDIRECT AUTO LENDING AND COMPLIANCE WITH THE EQUAL CREDIT OPPORTUNITY ACT (2013).

[42]   *See* Chapter III for a discussion of the legal theories of discrimination.

[43]   *See* CFPB Ally Consent Order, *supra* note 6.

44   Consent Order, United States v. Evergreen Bank Grp., No. 1:15-cv-04059 (N.D. Ill. May 7, 2015).

45   Richard Cordray, Director, Consumer Fin. Prot. Bureau., Prepared Remarks on the Payday/DAP Study Press Call (Apr. 24, 2013).

46   Consent Order, United States v. Nixon State Bank, No. 5:11-cv-00488-FB (W.D. Tex. June 21, 2011).

47   Consent Order, United States v. Fort Davis State Bank, No. 4:13-cv-00077-RAJ (W.D. Tex. Dec. 19, 2013).

48   Consent Order, United States v. First United Bank, No. 3:15-cv-00144-L (N.D. Tex. Jan. 15, 2015).

49   REBECCA BORNÉ & PETER SMITH, CTR. FOR RESPONSIBLE LENDING, BANK PAYDAY LENDING: THE STATE OF LENDING & ITS IMPACT ON U.S. HOUSEHOLDS 6 (2013); REBECCA BORNÉ ET AL., CTR. FOR RESPONSIBLE LENDING, BIG BANK PAYDAY LOANS: HIGH INTEREST LOANS THROUGH CHECKING ACCOUNTS KEEP CUSTOMERS IN LONG-TERM DEBT 8 (2011).

50   David Skanderson & Dubravka Ritter, *Fair Lending Analysis of Credit Cards* (Fed. Reserve Bank of Phila., Payment Cards Ctr. Discussion Paper No. 14-02, 2014).

51   Simon Firestone, *Race, Ethnicity, and Credit Card Marketing*, 46 J. OF MONEY, CREDIT & BANKING 1205 (2014).

52   CONSUMER FIN. PROT. BUREAU, EDUCATION LOAN EXAMINATION PROCEDURES 4 (2013).

53   *See, e.g., id.* at 10-12.

54   Joint Guidance on Overdraft Protection Programs, 70 Fed. Reg. 9,127, 9,131 (Feb. 24, 2005).

55   FED. DEPOSIT INS. CORP., FDIC LETTER NO. FIL-81-2010, OVERDRAFT PAYMENT PROGRAMS AND CONSUMER PROTECTION: FINAL OVERDRAFT PAYMENT SUPERVISORY GUIDANCE (2010).

56   *See* Conciliation Agreement, *supra* note 13.

57   *See* Press Release, *supra* note 14.

58   *See* ANDREA MITCHELL & LORI SOMMERFIELD, AM. ASS'N OF BANK DIRS., RED FLAGS FOR FAIR LENDING RISK - HOW BANKS CAN IDENTIFY AND

RESOLVE THEM (2012). Additional red flags include loan terms based on age differentiation, significant consumer complaints, negative examination or audit results, and changes in laws, rules, regulatory guidance, or regulatory expectations that make the products or services currently offered suspect.

[59]   CFPB White Paper, *supra* note 41.

[60]   *See* Agreed Order, *supra* note 9.

[61]   *See* Jo Ann Barefoot & Lori J. Sommerfield, *Regulatory Relationship Management: Planning, Organizing and Managing Examinations*, 96 BNA'S BANKING REP. 887 (May 10, 2011); Jo Ann Barefoot & Lori J. Sommerfield, *Regulatory Relationship Management: Building Trust, Credibility With Regulators*, 96 BNA BANKING REP. 18 (May 3, 2011).

[62]   *See also* Andrew Sandler, Andrea Mitchell & Susanna Khalil, *A Practical Guide to CFPB Compliance Examination Management*, 29 REV. OF BANKING & FIN. SERVS. 125 (Oct. 2013).

[63]   CFPB 2015 Fair Lending Report, *supra* note 40, at 9-10.

[64]   *Id.* at 9-11.

[65]   12 U.S.C. § 1828(x).

[66]   For additional information regarding LAR format, *see* FED. FIN. INSTS. EXAMINATION COUNCIL, A GUIDE TO HMDA REPORTING: GETTING IT RIGHT! (2013), http://www.ffiec.gov/hmda/pdf/2013guide.pdf.

[67]   For purposes of Regulation C, any lender that meets the definition of a "financial institution" (as defined in 12 C.F.R. § 1003.2) is required to collect HMDA data and file a LAR by March 1 of each calendar year. *See* 12 C.F.R. §§ 1003.4, 1003.5(a).

[68]   CONSUMER FIN. PROT. BUREAU, CFPB BULL. NO. 2013-11, HOME MORTGAGE DISCLOSURE ACT (HMDA) AND REGULATION C – COMPLIANCE MANAGEMENT; CFPB HMDA RESUBMISSION SCHEDULE AND GUIDELINES; AND HMDA ENFORCEMENT (2013).

[69]   For lenders reporting fewer than 100,000 LAR entries, HMDA data should be corrected and resubmitted when ten percent or more of a sample of HMDA LAR entries contain errors.

For lenders reporting 100,000 or more LAR entries, HMDA data should be corrected and resubmitted when four percent or more of a data sample contain errors. The threshold is lower for these lenders because they are considered to have a more significant impact on access to mortgage credit. In addition, for lenders reporting 100,000 or more LAR entries, resubmission of HMDA data may be required even if error rates are below four percent if the errors prevent an accurate analysis of the lender's lending activities.

For these HMDA LAR resubmission thresholds, *see* CONSUMER FIN. PROT. BUREAU, HMDA RESUBMISSION SCHEDULE AND GUIDELINES (2013), http://files.consumerfinance.gov/f/201310_cfpb_hmda_resubmission-guidelines_fair-lending.pdf.

70   Mortgage Master, Inc., CFPB No. 2013-CFPB-0006 (Oct. 9, 2013) [hereinafter CFPB Mortgage Master Consent Order]; Washington Federal, CFPB No. 2013-CFPB-0005 (Oct. 9, 2013) [hereinafter CFPB Washington Federal Consent Order].

71   The CFPB Consent Order for Washington Federal, *supra* note 71, requires the board of directors to (i) review all submissions required by the Consent Order prior to submission to the CFPB; (ii) authorize and adopt actions as needed for the bank to perform its obligations under the Consent Order; (iii) require timely reporting by management of actions required to be taken by the bank under the Consent Order; and (iv) take corrective action in a timely and appropriate manner for any material non-compliance with such actions.

72   12 C.F.R. § 1003.6(b)(1).

73   633 F. Supp. 2d 922 (N.D. Cal. 2008).

74   *Ramirez v. GreenPoint Mortg. Funding, Inc.,* 268 F.R.D. 627 (N.D. Cal. 2010).

75   Conciliation Agreement, between Metro. St. Louis Equal Hous. Opportunity Council and First Nat'l Bank of St. Louis, FHEO No. 07-10-0152-8 (Dec. 21, 2010).

76   Home Mortgage Disclosure (Regulation C), 79 Fed. Reg. 51,732 (proposed Aug. 29, 2014) [hereinafter CFPB Proposed Rule, Regulation C]; Home Mortgage Disclosure (Regulation C), 80 Fed. Reg. 66,128 (Oct. 28, 2015) [hereinafter CFPB Final Rule, Regulation C].

[77] The tool is available on the CFPB's website at http://www.consumerfinance.gov/hmda/.

[78] CFPB 2014 Fair Lending Report, *supra* note 40, at 4, 14.

[79] 12 C.F.R. § 1002.5, 1002.13.

[80] 12 C.F.R. § 1003.4.

[81] 12 C.F.R. § 1003.1(b)(iii).

[82] *See* Chapter VII and Appendix C for more information on HMDA requirements.

[83] 12 C.F.R. § 1002.5(b); *see* Settlement Agreement & Order, United States v. Fidelity Fed. Bank, FSB, No. 1:02-cv-03906 (E.D.N.Y. July 25, 2002).

[84] CFPB Ally Consent Order, *supra* note 6; Consent Order, United States v. Ally Fin. Inc., No. 2:13-cv-15180 (E.D. Mich. Dec. 23, 2013); American Honda Finance Corporation, CFPB No. 2015-CFPB-0014 (July 14, 2015); Consent Order, United States v. Am. Honda Fin. Corp., No. 2:15-cv-05264 (C.D. Cal. July 16, 2015); Fifth Third Bank, CFPB No. 2015-CFPB-0024 (Sept. 28, 2015); Consent Order, United States v. Fifth Third Bank, No. 1:15-cv-626 (S.D. Ohio Sept. 28, 2015).

[85] Marc N. Elliott et al., *Using the Census Bureau's Surname List to Improve Estimates of Race/Ethnicity and Associated Disparities*, 9 HEALTH SERVS. & OUTCOMES RESEARCH METHODOLOGY 69 (Apr. 10, 2009).

[86] CFPB White Paper, *supra* note 41.

[87] Elliott et al., *supra* note 86.

[88] ARTHUR P. BAINES & DR. MARSHA J. COURCHANE, AM. FIN. SERVS. ASS'N, FAIR LENDING: IMPLICATIONS FOR THE INDIRECT AUTO FINANCE MARKET (2014).

[89] *Id.* at 56.

[90] *Id.*

[91] FED. FIN. INSTS. EXAMINATION COUNCIL, *supra* note 19, at app. 19.

[92] CONSUMER FIN. PROT. BUREAU, CFPB BULL. NO. 2013-06, RESPONSIBLE BUSINESS CONDUCT: SELF-POLICING, SELF-REPORTING, REMEDIATION AND COOPERATION (2013).

[93]   12 C.F.R. § 1080.6(c).

[94]   12 C.F.R. § 1080.6(e).

[95]   Under CFPB rules, "[i]f the [CID] seeks [electronically stored information ("ESI")], the recipient shall ensure that a person familiar with its ESI systems and methods of retrieval participates in the [meet and confer]." 12 C.F.R. § 1080.6(c)(2).

[96]   12 C.F.R. § 1080.6(g).

[97]   With the CFPB, for example, this is called a PARR letter in the event of a preliminary supervisory determination or a Notice and Opportunity to Respond and Advise ("NORA") letter in the event of an investigation arising out of the enforcement division. As noted above, the prudential regulators typically issue a 15-day letter.

[98]   Equal Credit Opportunity Act, Pub. L. No. 93-495, § 502, 88 Stat. 1521 (1974) (emphasis added).

[99]   Equal Credit Opportunity Act Amendments of 1976, Pub. L. No. 94-239, § 2, 90 Stat. 251 (1976).

[100]   15 U.S.C. § 1691(a)(1)-(3). A creditor means "a person who, in the ordinary course of business, regularly participates in a credit decision, including setting the terms of the credit." 12 C.F.R. § 1002.2(*l*).

[101]   12 C.F.R. pt. 202, supp. I (Fed. Reserve Bd., Div. of Consumer & Cmty. Affairs, Official Staff Interpretations 2011).

[102]   133 S. Ct. 2675 (2013).

[103]   Memorandum from CFPB Director Richard Cordray to CFPB Staff (June 25, 2014) [hereinafter CFPB Memorandum], http://files.consumerfinance.gov/f/201407_cfpb_memo_ensuring-equal-treatment-for-same-sex-married-couples.pdf. It is noteworthy that the CFPB's guidance took the unusual form of a memorandum to CFPB staff, rather than in a bulletin or as an interpretive release subject to the Administrative Procedure Act's public and notice requirements. In February 2014, DOJ also issued a memorandum to its employees. Memorandum from the Attorney General to All Department of Justice Employees, Department Policy on Ensuring Equal Treatment for Same-Sex Married Couples (Feb. 10, 2014).

[104]   Windsor, 133 S. Ct. at 2683 (quoting 1 U.S.C. § 7).

[105]   CFPB Memorandum, *supra* note 104, at 1.

[106]   15 U.S.C. § 1691c(c).

[107]   15 U.S.C. § 1691e.

[108]   15 U.S.C. § 1691e(g).

[109]   12 U.S.C. § 5514(c)(3)

[110]   Despite the narrower circumstances in which violations are required to be referred to DOJ under ECOA (*see* 15 U.S.C. § 1691e(g)), the prudential regulators and the CFPB generally refer all potential pattern or practice discrimination matters to the DOJ.

[111]   *See generally* 42 U.S.C. §§ 3608-3612 (HUD administration and enforcement of the FHA); 42 U.S.C. § 3614 (DOJ enforcement of the FHA).

[112]   Exec. Order No. 12,892, 59 Fed. Reg. 2,939 (Jan. 17, 1994).

[113]   Equal Access to Housing in HUD Programs Regardless of Sexual Orientation or Gender Identity, 77 Fed. Reg. 5,662 (Feb. 3, 2012).

[114]   Bank of America, N.A., HUD No. 12-1657-MR (Nov. 1, 2012).

[115]   Implementation of the Fair Housing Act's Discriminatory Effects Standard, 78 Fed. Reg. 11,460 (Feb. 15, 2013).

[116]   42 U.S.C. § 3614(a).

[117]   42 U.S.C. § 3610(a)(1)(A).

[118]   42 U.S.C. § 3610(a)(1)(A); 42 U.S.C. § 3612(o).

[119]   12 U.S.C. §§ 2801–2809.

[120]   This information includes the applicant's age; the applicant's credit score; the total annual percentage rate associated with the loan and a benchmark rate for all loans; the value of the collateral pledged for the loan; the presence of contractual terms that would allow payments that are not fully amortizing; and the number of months after which an introductory rate can change. These enhanced collection and reporting requirements will come into effect after the CFPB publishes rules to implement these changes. Dodd-Frank Act, Pub. L. 111-203, § 1094, 124

Stat. 1376, 2097 (2010).

[121]   See CFPB Proposed Rule, Regulation C, *supra* note 77.

[122]   See CFPB Final Rule, Regulation C, *supra* note 77.

[123]   Home Mortgage Disclosure (Regulation C) Adjustment to Asset-Size Exemption Threshold, 79 Fed. Reg. 77,854 (Dec. 29, 2014).

[124]   12 C.F.R. § 1003.2 (definition of "financial institution," paragraph (1)).

[125]   CFPB Mortgage Master Consent Order, *supra* note 71; CFPB Washington Federal Consent Order, *supra* note 71; CONSUMER FIN. PROT. BUREAU, *supra* note 69.

[126]   FED. FIN. INSTS. EXAMINATION COUNCIL, *supra* note 67.

[127]   The CFPB has expanded its interpretation of responsible lending laws by ensuring that banking financial products and services provide value to consumers commensurate with the costs. For example, one of the CFPB's recurring enforcement action themes has been ensuring that credit card "add-on products," such as debt protection, identity theft protection, and credit scoring tracking, represent fair value to consumers.

In conjunction with the CFPB's first credit card add-on product enforcement action in 2012, the Bureau released Bulletin 2012-06, which signaled to the industry that the CFPB was looking very closely at UDAAP issues in marketing and sales practices in the credit card markets. CONSUMER FIN. PROT. BUREAU, CFPB BULL. NO. 2012-06, MARKETING OF CREDIT CARD ADD-ON PRODUCTS (July 18, 2012). Implied within that guidance is the concept that consumers should receive real value for the add-on products they agree to purchase. Therefore, banks that market and sell credit card add-on products should closely review that guidance and evaluate their own practices to take corrective action as needed. Particular consideration should be given to processes for assessing whether a product or service and its terms and conditions provide fair, tangible value to consumers and satisfy regulatory concerns about the potential for consumer harm.

[128]   12 U.S.C. § 45.

[129]   12 U.S.C. §§ 5531, 5536. We also note that the Servicemembers Civil

Relief Act ("SCRA") is at times considered a "responsible lending" law. 50 U.S.C. §§ 3901, 4043. The SCRA, which was amended by Congress in 2003, is designed to ease certain financial burdens for servicemembers on active duty military service. The SCRA is not addressed in this Handbook. By statute, only the DOJ has express authority to enforce the SCRA. *See* 50 U.S.C. § 4041. The prudential regulators, CFPB, FTC, and Department of Defense ("DOD"), however, are also actively concerned with servicemember protections involving financial products and services. The prudential regulators, CFPB, and FTC may refer cases to the DOJ for enforcement, work in coordination with the DOJ on enforcement actions, or even take affirmative action on their own to enforce SCRA despite the lack of express statutory authority. In fact, the CFPB appears to be enforcing SCRA-type protections under a UDAAP theory.

[130] For example, CFPB Director Richard Cordray explained during Congressional testimony in 2012 that the determination of what practices are abusive "is going to have to be a fact and circumstances issue," and that it would "not be useful to try to define a term like that in the abstract." *How Will the CFPB Function Under Richard Cordray: Hearing before the Subcomm. on TARP, Fin. Servs., and Bailouts of Pub. & Private Programs*, 112th Cong. 112-107 (2012) (statement of Richard Cordray, Director, Consumer Fin. Prot. Bureau).

Since 2012, the CFPB has undertaken several enforcement actions involving abusive practices. In one case, for example, the CFPB alleged that Ace Cash Express, Inc. ("Ace") used illegal debt collection tactics with respect to its payday lending services. Specifically, the Bureau alleged that Ace engaged in abusive conduct by creating an "artificial sense of urgency" to pressure delinquent consumers to pay off their existing payday loans and then immediately take out a new payday loan with accompanying fees, even though borrowers had already demonstrated an inability to repay. The CFPB believed these tactics took unreasonable advantage of the inability of consumers to protect their own interests in selecting or using a consumer financial product or service. Ace agreed to pay $5 million in consumer restitution and a $5 million civil money penalty. Ace Cash Express, Inc., CFPB No. 2014-CFPB-0008 (July 8, 2014).

[131] *See, e.g.,* U.S. Bank National Association, Cincinnati, Ohio, CFPB

No. 2013-CFPB-0003 (June 26, 2013) (alleging violations of the Truth in Lending Act/Regulation Z and UDAAP); Flagstar Bank, F.S.B., CFPB No. 2014-CFPB-0014 (Sept. 29, 2014) (alleging violations of the loss mitigation provisions of RESPA's Mortgage Servicing Final Rule and UDAAP); Manufacturers and Traders Trust Company, CFPB No. 2014-CFPB-0016 (Oct. 9, 2014) (alleging violations of the Truth in Savings Act/Regulation DD and UDAAP).

Made in the USA
Middletown, DE
22 May 2016